IMMORTALITY

LORAINE BOETTNER

AUTHOR OF

Studies in Theology
The Reformed Doctrine of Predestination
The Millennium
Roman Catholicism

THE PRESBYTERIAN AND REFORMED PUBLISHING CO.
PHILADELPHIA, PENNSYLVANIA

IMMORTALITY
by Loraine Boettner

Copyright, 1956 by
Loraine Boettner

Eighth printing, April, 1969

*More than thirty thousand copies in print, including translations in
Spanish, Italian, Portuguese, Japanese, Chinese and Korean*

Contents

III. THE INTERMEDIATE STATE

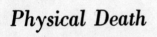

Physical Death

I. Physical Death

1. The Certainty and Reality of Death

Death and the future state are by their very nature mysteries incapable of solution apart from the revelation that has been given in Scripture. There is a tendency on the part of many people to avoid any serious discussion or even thought on the subject of death. Yet every person knows that in the normal course of events sooner or later that experience will happen to him. Every community has its cemetery. Nothing is more certain about life than the fact of death. It may be long delayed, but it will surely come. All human history and experience point to that conclusion. It has been demonstrated a thousand times in the lives of those about us who have been called from among the living. Heart attacks and other diseases, accidents, wars, fires, etc., have taken their toll. Death is no respecter of persons. It may come to any one, young or old, rich or poor, saint or sinner, at any time or any place. And when God calls none can escape, nor excuse, nor alibi that appointment.

Divine revelation solemnly states that, "It is appointed unto men once to die, and after this cometh judgment," Heb. 9:27. Truly life is short, death is sure, and eternity is long.

We set out on the journey of life with high hopes and soaring ambitions. Life seems rosy and death seems far away. Year after year life runs its accustomed course, smoothly and serenely. We read of thousands dying from starvation in India, and of other thousands that drown in China; but those places are far away and the people are not known to us. A neighbor down the street dies. That

9

causes us to stop and think. We send flowers and feel sorry for the family. But still it does not affect us directly, and we soon continuue with our work and play. There develops within us a sense of immunity to tragedy and death.

Then suddenly the bottom drops out of *our* world. Perhaps a mother or father, or some other relative or friend, is taken, leaving an aching void. Many of us have already had that experience. We have watched the changing face and have listened helplessly to the shortening breath. We have spoken or looked the last good-bye, and then, in an instant, the departing one has passed out of sight and out of hearing, into the world of the unknown. The body which, perhaps only yesterday, was so full of life and animation now lies before us an insensate piece of clay. A short time ago the one we loved was here, going about his work or speaking to us; and now, perhaps in one moment, he is gone — gone so very, very far away. What baffling thoughts rush in upon the mind in those moments pressing for an answer! But there is no answer in either reason or experience. The Bible alone has an answer for the thoughts that come with such perplexity and insistence.

At such a time it may be that, as has been said in a recent helpful booklet, "The stricken father loses his faith, or the broken-hearted mother cries out, 'Why did this have to happen to me?' It is hard to answer such questions to the satisfaction and comfort of those who ask it, for the simple reason that at such a time those who ask it are not normal. It is difficult for the mind that is shocked beyond comprehension to be reasonable. The breaking heart wants none of your logic. It wants comfort and peace. Above all, it wants to turn back the page, to recall the life that has sped — and this cannot be. Death is so permanent. There is no recall. It comes to you and yours as it has come to millions of others — it is inevitable. It may come as a thief in the night, or it may approach slowly after ample warning. It may come early in life, or after years of happiness. But come it must.   The only way to escape it is never to be born."[1]

Vital statistics inform us that the world's population is about two and one-half billion (United Nations statistical yearbook, 1954), and that of this number approximately thirty million die every year.   That means that on an average one person somewhere in the world dies every second. Think of it! Every time the clock ticks some one dies! 60 die every minute, 3600 every hour, and 86,400 every day. And except for a very few each of those leaves some heart torn and mourning.   Your appointed time, and mine, has not come yet.   But it will be somewhere on that timetable.

The Apostle Peter expresses this general truth with a melancholy eloquence: "For all flesh is as grass, and all the glory thereof as the flower of grass.   The grass withereth, and the flower falleth: but the word of the Lord abideth for ever," I Peter 1:24,25.   We would point out that not only individuals but even nations and civilizations have their periods of growth and dominance, and of decline and oblivion.   History is quite clear in showing that one nation after another has temporarily dominated the world scene, and then disappeared.   Assyria, Babylon, Persia, Egypt, Greece, Rome, Napoleon's French Empire, the Third Reich, — one by one these have had their day of glory and then have become merely historical names.   Arnold Toynbee in his great work, *A Study of History*, points out that from the dawn of history until the present time there have been twenty-one distinct civilizations, only seven of which survive as world forces.

The poet Shelley, in one of his writings, describes an oriental ruin bearing this inscription:

"My name is Ozymandias, king of kings;
Look on my works, ye mighty, and despair."

---

1. *For Those Who Mourn*, p. 4. Anonymous.

But, continues the poet,

"Nothing besides remains. Round the decay
Of that colossal wreck, boundless and bare,
The lone and level sands stretch far away."

2. The Penalty for Sin

The essential truth that we should keep in mind about death is that it is the penalty for sin. Repeatedly the Bible drives home that teaching. It is not just the natural end of life. It holds its awful sway over us and we are doomed to die because we are sinners. When man was first created he was placed on a test of pure obedience. He was commanded not to eat of the tree of knowledge of good and evil, and the penalty for disobedience was announced in these words: "In the day that thou eatest thereof thou shalt surely die," Gen. 2:17.

Adam deliberately and wilfully disobeyed God's command, and in so doing he in effect transferred his allegiance from God to the Devil. Having thereby shown that he was not a loyal and obedient citizen, but a rebel, in the kingdom, there was no alternative but that the threatened penalty should be executed. The Bible thus makes it clear that death is a penal evil, that is, an evil inflicted in accordance with law and as a penalty. This teaching is repeated in the prophets: "The soul that sinneth, it shall die," Ezek. 18:4; and in the New Testament it is connected with the fall in Adam: "As through one man sin entered into the world, and death through sin; and so death passed unto all men, for that all sinned," Rom. 5:12; "In Adam all die," I Cor. 15:22; and again, "The wages of sin is death," Rom. 6:23. Death therefore does not come merely as a result of natural law, as the Unitarians and Modernists would have us believe. Rather, had there been no sin, there would have been no death.

How grateful we should be that God has given us some revelation concerning the cause and effect of death. Not everything is revealed that might be required to satisfy our curiosity, but enough is revealed that the mysterious aspects concerning it are largely cleared up and the dread in large measure removed. We have read various explanations of death, but we are convinced that there is none so true and accurate as that given in the Bible.

The sentence imposed as a result of Adam's sin included much more than the dissolution of the body. The word "death" as used in the Scriptures in reference to the effects of sin includes every form of evil that is inflicted in its punishment. It meant the opposite of the reward promised, which was blessed and eternal life in heaven. It meant, therefore, the eternal miseries of hell (which is also the fate of the fallen angels or demons), together with the fore-taste of those miseries which are felt in the evils that are suffered in this life. Its nature can be seen in part in the effects of sin which actually have fallen upon the human race. Its immediate and lasting effect was to cause sin rather than holiness to become man's natural element so that in his unregenerate state he seeks to avoid even the thought of God and holy things. The Scriptures declare him to be "dead" in "trespasses and sins," Eph. 2:1, in which state he is as unable to understand and appreciate the offer of redemption through faith in Christ as a physically dead man is to hear the sounds of this world.

The whole Christian world, Protestant, Roman Catholic and Greek Catholic alike, has believed that in the fall Adam, as the divinely appointed head of the race, stood representative of the entire race, and that he brought this evil not only upon himself but upon all his posterity. Dr. Charles Hodge has expressed this connection very clearly in the following words: "In virtue of the union, federal and natural, between Adam and his posterity, his sin, although not their act, is so imputed to them that it is the judicial ground of the penalty threatened against him coming also on them. . . . To impute sin, in Scriptural and theological language, is to impute the guilt of sin. And by guilt is meant not criminality, nor moral ill-desert, nor demerit, much less moral pollution, but judicial obligation to satisfy justice."[2]

Paul sets forth this doctrine of the imputation of Adam's sin and also the kindred doctrine of the imputation of Christ's righteousness to us when he says: "For as through one man's disobedience the many were made sinners, even so through the obedience of the one shall the many be made righteous," Rom. 5:19; and again, "For as in Adam all die, so also in Christ shall all be made alive," I Cor. 15:22.

In accordance with this we find that even infants, who have no personal sin, nevertheless suffer pain and death. Now the Scriptures uniformly represent suffering and death as the wages of sin. God would be unjust if He executed the penalty on those who are not guilty. Since the penalty falls on infants, they must be guilty; and since they have not personally committed sin, they must, as the Scripture says, be guilty of Adam's sin. All those who have inherited human nature from Adam, that is, all of his descendants, were in him as the fruit is in the germ, and have, as it were, grown up one person with him. In the system of redemption that God has provided we are redeemed through Christ in precisely the same way that we fell in Adam, — that is, through a Substitute who stands as our federal head and representative and who acts in our stead. It is utterly illogical to believe in salvation through Christ without believing also in the fall through Adam.

In regard to the connection between sin and death Dr. Louis Berkhof, Professor Emeritus of Calvin Seminary, has well said:

"Pelagians and Socinians teach that man was created mortal, not merely in the sense that he could fall a prey to death, but in the sense that he was, in virtue of his creation, under the law of death, and in course of time was bound to die. This means that Adam was not only suscep-

---

2. *Systematic Theology*, II p. 120.

tible to death, but was actually subject to it before he fell.
The advocates of this view were prompted primarily by the
desire to evade the proof for original sin derived from the
suffering and death of infants. Present day science seems
to support this position by stressing the fact that death is
the law of organized matter, since it carries within it the
seeds of decay and dissolution. . . . Suppose that science
had proved conclusively that death reigned in the vegetable
and animal world before the entrance of sin, then it would
not necessarily follow that it also prevailed in the world
of rational and moral beings. And even if it were established beyond the shadow of a doubt that all physical or-
ganisms, the human included, now carry within them the
seeds of dissolution, this would not yet prove that man was
not an exception to the rule before the fall. Shall we say
that the almighty power of God, by which the universe
was created, was not sufficient to continue man in life indefinitely? Moreover we ought to bear in mind the following Scriptural data: (1) Man was created in the image of
God and this, in view of the perfect condition in which the
image of God existed originally, would seem to exclude the
possibility of his carrying within him the seeds of dissolution and mortality. (2) Physical death is not represented
in Scripture as the natural result of the continuation of the
original condition of man, due to his failure to rise to the
height of immortality by the path of obedience; but as the
result of his spiritual death, Rom. 6:23; I Cor. 15:56;
James 1:15. (3) Scriptural expressions certainly point to
death as something introduced into the world of humanity
by sin, and as a positive punishment for sin, Gen. 2:17;
Rom. 5:12,17; 6:23; I Cor. 15:21; James 1:15. (4) Death
is not represented as something natural to the life of man,
a mere falling short of an ideal, but very definitely as
something foreign and hostile to human life; it is an expression of divine anger, Ps. 90:7,11, a judgment, Rom.
1:32, a condemnation, Rom. 5:16, and a curse, Gal. 3:13,
and fills the hearts of the children of men with dread and

fear, just because it is felt to be something unnatural. All this does not mean, however, that there may not have been death in some sense of the word in the lower creation apart from sin, but even there the entrance of sin evidently brought a bondage of corruption that was foreign to the creature, Rom. 8:20-22."[3]

That the penalty threatened upon Adam was not primarily physical death is shown by the fact that he did not die physically for some 930 years after the fall. But he did die spiritually the very moment he fell. He died just as really as the fish dies when taken from the water, or as the plant dies when taken from the soil. He was immediately alienated from God, and was cast out of the garden of Eden.

But even in regard to physical death, that also in a sense was immediately executed. For though our first parents lived many years, they immediately began to grow old. Since the fall, life has been an unceasing march toward the grave.

3. Three Kinds of Death: Spiritual — Physical — Eternal

1. *Spiritual death* means the separation or alienation of the soul from God. It is in principle the condition in which the Devil and the demons are, but since in this world man's descent into evil is restrained to some extent by common grace, it has not yet proceeded to such a degree of depravity as is found in them. This was the primary penalty threatened against Adam in the Garden of Eden. Since man can only truly live when in communion with God, spiritual death means his complete undoing and the continual worsening of his condition. It means that while man may still perform many acts which are good in themselves, his works never merit salvation because they are not done with right motives toward God. Spiritual death, like a poisoned fountain, pollutes the whole stream of life, and

3. *Systematic Theology*, p. 669.

were it not for the restraining influence of common grace ordinary human life would become a hell on earth.

The opposite of spiritual death is spiritual life. It was this to which Jesus referred when He said to Martha: "I am the resurrection, and the life: he that believeth on me, though he die, yet shall he live; and whosoever liveth and believeth on me shall never die," John 11:25, 26. And again, "He that heareth my word, and believeth him that sent me, hath eternal life, and cometh not into judgment, but hath passed out of death into life," John 5:24.

2. *Physical death* means the separation of the soul from the body. This, too, is a part of the penalty for sin, although, as indicated in the preceding section, it is not the most important part. In contrast with the angels, man was created with a dual nature, a spirit united with a body. He receives information through the avenues of sense. His body is the organ through which he makes contact with other human beings and with the world about him. When he dies he loses that contact, and, so far as we know, the spirits of the departed have no further contact with the living nor with the world about us. We do not know what the process is by which angels, who are pure spirits, communicate with each other, but presumably it is direct communication without intervening means, similar to what we refer to as thought transference or intuitive knowledge. At any rate the Bible gives no reason to believe that the dead can communicate with the living, but quite the contrary. (The alleged communications through spiritualistic mediums will be discussed in a later section.)

At death man's body, which is composed of some thirty different chemical elements, returns to the earth from which it was taken. This phase of death, too, was conquered by Christ when He made atonement for the sins of His people, for they eventually receive a gloriously restored resurrection body.

3. *Eternal death* is spiritual death made permanent. "This," says Dr. Berkhof, "may be regarded as the culmination and completion of spiritual death. The restraints of the present fall away, and the corruption of sin has its perfect work. The full weight of the wrath of God descends on the condemned. Their separation from God, the source of life and joy, is complete, and this means death in the most awful sense of the word. Their outward condition is made to correspond with the inward state of their evil souls. There are pangs of conscience and physical pain. 'And the smoke of their torment goeth up for ever and ever.' Rev. 14:11."[4]

The first death is physical, and it awaits every human being. The second death is spiritual, and it awaits only those who are outside of Christ. It is the eternal separation of the individual from God, and it results in the eternal punishment of those whose names are not written in the book of life (Rev. 20:12-15). In another connection the Bible speaks of a new birth, which in reality is a spiritual re-birth: "Ye must be born anew," John 3:3,7. Those who are born only once, the physical birth, die twice, a physical and a spiritual or eternal death. Those who are born twice die only once, the physical death. These latter are the Lord's redeemed.

Looked at merely in itself and from the standpoint of the world death is, as Dr. Hodge says, "the event of all others the most to be dreaded." He goes on to say that, "As the love of life is natural and instinctive, so is the fear of death. It is, however, not only instinctive, it is rational. It is the end of the only kind of existence of which we have any consciousness or experience. To the eye of sense, it is annihilation. The dead, to all appearances, are as non-existent as the unborn. Death means the loss of all our possessions, of all sources of enjoyment to which we have been

---

4. *Ibid.*, p. 261.

accustomed. It is the sundering of all social ties, the final separation of parents and children.

"Though to the eye of sense death is annihilation, it is not so to the eye of reason or of conscience. Such is the intellectual and moral nature of man, that all men have the apprehension or conviction of a state of conscious existence after death. But what that state is, human reason cannot tell. The torch of science and the lamp of philosophy are extinguished at the grave. The soul at death enters upon the unknown, the dark, the boundless, the endless.

"These, however, are not the considerations which render death so terrible. The sting of death is sin. Sin, of necessity, involves guilt, and guilt is a fearful looking for of judgment. To the guilty, therefore, death is, must be, and ought to be, the king of terrors. There are men so stupid that they die as the ox dies. There are others so reckless that they fear not to challenge God to do His worst. Multitudes are in such a state of lethargy at the approach of death that they have no apprehension. These facts do not alter the case. It remains true that for a sinner unreconciled to God, death is the most dreadful of all events, and is so regarded just in proportion as the soul is duly enlightened."[5]

The only possible way by which the terrors of death can be diverted is for the person to be freed from his burden of sin. But God cannot merely issue a pardon for sin and set it aside as if it were of no consequence. In the beginning He made the law that the penalty should be death. That was no idle threat. It was rather a statement of the moral law, and was based on His own nature. It is in fact a transcript of His nature, and is therefore immutable and inexorable. The demands of His law are the demands of His holy nature. But how, then, are those demands to be met? To that end men have sought to earn their own salvation by sacrifices, by asceticism, by good works and self disci-

5. *Conference Papers*, p. 257.

pline, by prayer and fasting and church rituals, but to no
avail. Man in himself simply cannot pay the debt of sin.

But what we could not do for ourselves God has done for
us. As our Substitute and for our salvation Christ became
incarnate, took our human nature upon Himself, took our
place as the offender before His own law, and by His own
suffering and death upon the cross, bore the penalty for
sin that was due to us. This we call His "passive" obedience. Also as our Substitute and by His perfect obedience
to the moral law He lived a sinless life during the thirty-
three years that He was on earth and earned for us the
blessings of eternal life. This we call His "active" obedience. Each of these phases of His work was necessary for
our salvation. And because He was Deity incarnate and
therefore a person of infinite value and dignity, His obedience to the law and His suffering were of infinite value,
and were therefore the means by which God might save as
vast a multitude as He saw fit to call to Himself. The moral
relationship between God and His people was thus restored, and as a consequence His people are cleansed of
their sin and transformed by the Holy Spirit into His
image.

As a result of the redemption accomplished by Christ the
death of the body becomes for His people the gateway to
heaven, a transition by which they move out of the body
and into the presence of the Lord. It has lost its sting.
"Death is swallowed up in victory," I Cor. 15:54.

4. The Christian Still Subject to Physical Death

A further problem arises concerning the suffering and
death of believers, and it is this: If their sins have been
atoned for, why is it still necessary for them to die? Why
is this part of the penalty still executed? Why are they not
transferred from earth to heaven in somewhat the same
way that Enoch and Elijah were taken up? It is perfectly
evident that even the best of God's people do suffer and die,

their sufferings sometimes being far in excess of those which befall others who are notoriously wicked.

The answer is that the suffering and death that falls on believers is not, strictly speaking, penal, — that is, it is not suffering inflicted as a punishment for sin. All true punishment for their sins was borne by Christ. These sufferings are rather disciplinary measures or chastisements, sufferings designed for the moral and spiritual advancement of those who experience them. The death of believers also serves as a warning to all those still in this life that the time of their death is also approaching. The death of the wicked, however, is truly penal, a consequence of and a punishment for sin. The death of the believer and that of the unbeliever may appear outwardly to be the same, but from the divine viewpoint there is a great difference.

Dr. Robert L. Dabney, an outstanding Southern theologian, has set forth this problem quite fully. Says he:

"Although believers are fully justified, yet according to that plan of grace which God has seen fit to adopt, bodily death is a necessary and wholesome chastisement for the good of the believer's soul. A chastisement, while God's motive in it is only benevolent, does not cease to be, to the believer, a real natural evil in itself, and to be felt as such. God wisely and kindly exercises in chastisements His divine prerogative of bringing good out of evil. Hence chastisement is a means of spiritual benefit appropriate only to the sinning children of God. It would not be just, for instance, that God should adopt chastisement as a means to advance Gabriel, who never had any guilt, to some higher state of sanctified capabilities and blessedness; because where there is no guilt there can be no suffering. . . .

"A vicarious satisfaction [such as that made by Christ for His people] is not a commercial equivalent for their guilt, not a legal tender such as brings our Divine Creditor under a righteous obligation to cancel our whole indebtedness. But His acceptance of it as a legal satisfaction was, on His part, an act of pure grace; and therefore the acceptance acquits us just as far as, and no farther than, God is pleased to allow it." [To state this truth in other words we may say that the merits or fruits of Christ's atonement are not all made immediately available to His people, but are apportioned to them in due time, in accordance with the terms of the Covenant of Redemption which was entered into by the Father and the Son before the work of redemption was undertaken.] "And we learn from His word that He has been pleased to accept it just thus far; that the believer shall be required to pay no more penal satisfaction to the broken law; yet shall be liable to such suffering or chastisement as shall be wholesome for his own improvement, and appropriate to his sinning condition.

"The prospect of death serves, from the earliest day when it begins to stir the sinner's conscience to a wholesome seriousness, through all his convictions, conversion, Christian warfare, to humble his proud soul, to mortify carnality, to check pride, to foster spiritual mindedness. It is the fact that sicknesses are premonitions of death, which make them active means of sanctification. Bereavements through death of friends form another valuable class of disciplinary sufferings. And when the closing scene approaches, no doubt in every case where the believer is conscious, the pains of its approach, the solemn thoughts and emotions it suggests, are all used by the Holy Ghost as powerful means of sanctification to ripen the soul rapidly for heaven. . . . A race of sinners must be a race of mortals; death is the only check potent enough to prevent depravity from breaking out with a power which would make the state of the world perfectly intolerable!"[6]

Thus while sickness and death in themselves remain natural evils for the righteous and are dreaded by them as such, they are nevertheless in the economy of grace made subservient to their spiritual advancement and to the best interests of the kingdom of God.

---

6. *Theology*, pp. 818, 819.

But for the wicked death remains as much a penalty as it ever was. For them it means the end of their false sense of security, and an overwhelming, sudden destruction which they cannot escape. What utter loneliness must seize upon the unbeliever who has to leave friends and old associations in this world and go all alone into that mysterious future! How awful to go down into the valley of death without a Saviour!

Another point to be remembered in connection with either the penal or disciplinary character of death is that since we all are members of a fallen race God has the sovereign right to inflict that discipline or execute that penalty at whatever time He sees fit. He may, and often does, inflict it upon infants. If He delays the sentence until early youth, or middle age, or perhaps until old age, that is purely a matter of His mercy and grace. Without regard to moral character or personal achievements one life may drag on for many years in misery and disease while the Reaper tarries, while another no better nor any worse lives in health and wealth and meets an easy death. The very inequality and irrationality of death should teach us the gravity of our sin and the absolute sovereignty of God in executing the penalty whenever He chooses. It is not for us to say when our time shall come. When one is taken we should be thankful that the lives of so many others who were in the same condition have been spared. It is our duty to be prepared for that event whenever it may come, knowing that sooner or later it is sure to come.

5. The Christian Attitude Toward Death

"And I heard a voice from heaven saying, Write, Blessed are the dead who die in the Lord from henceforth: yea, saith the Spirit, that they may rest from their labors; for their works do follow them," Rev. 14:13.

"But I am in a strait betwixt the two, having the desire to depart and be with Christ; for it is very far better; yet

to abide in the flesh is more needful for your sake," Phil.
1:23.

*"Being therefore always of good courage, and knowing
that whilst we are at home in the body, we are absent from
the Lord (for we walk by faith, not by sight); we are of
good courage, I say, and are willing rather to be absent
from the body, and to be at home with the Lord,"* II Cor.
5:6-8.

*"Precious in the sight of Jehovah is the death of his
saints,"* Ps. 116:15.

"For me to live is Christ, and to die is gain," Phil. 1:21.

*"For we know that if the earthly house of our tabernacle
be dissolved, we have a building from God, a house not
made with hands, eternal in the heavens,"* II Cor. 5:1.

In his old age Paul wrote: *"For I am already being offered, and the time of my departure is come. I have fought
the good fight, I have finished the course, I have kept the
faith: henceforth there is laid up for me the crown of
righteousness, which the Lord, the righteous judge shall
give to me in that day; and not to me only, but also to all
of them that have loved his appearing,"* II Tim. 4:6-8.

Death holds no terrors for the true Christian. He sees
it rather as the boundary line between this world and the
next, or as the portal through which His Lord entered to
prepare the way and through which he now follows. He is
prepared, watchful, sober, knowing that his appointed salvation is sure, and that when his Lord comes it will be for
the purpose of leading him into his inheritance. The day of
his death becomes in fact his coronation day. It means
leaving a world of sin and sorrow, of pain and disappointment, of toil and hardship, and entering into a far better
world, a world of holiness and blessedness, of happiness
and freedom and accomplishment, and of direct fellowship
with God. In comparison with the present world the future
and eternal world is by all odds to be preferred. In fact so
great is the contrast that we may even say that the terres-

tial life, as compared with the celestial, is of no value at all.

Paul's comforting description, "absent from the body . . . at home with the Lord," seems to mean that death is a moving out of the earthly tabernacle of our physical body and into a heavenly abode. For Jesus death meant returning to the Father: "Now I go unto him that sent me," John 16:5. It is therefore not the end of life, but rather the beginning of a far more wonderful and glorious existence than can possibly be experienced here. The grave is no longer seen as a blind alley that blocks all human progress, but as a thoroughfare through which man advances to a far better world. He no longer seeks for the living among the dead, no longer thinks of his deceased loved one as lying there in the casket or in the grave, but as having departed completely from the old body and as being alive for ever more.

Commenting on the words of Paul to Timothy (quoted above), Dr. Samuel McP. Glasgow says: "How gracious and magnificent, how glorious and radiant with promise, is Paul's view of life at its far end and his verdict upon the closing days of our earthly chapter! Behind him is a life of almost unequaled activity, — going, giving, speaking, serving, suffering. He is now in prison. He senses that the end of life is at hand. For him it holds no terrors whatsoever. Under these circumstances we hear him speak and give an old man's verdict on life and his evaluation of its closing days."[7]

For the Christian there are two aspects of death that must always be kept in balance. On the one hand, death has been so transformed by the atonement wrought by Christ that its sting has been removed and it comes now as the last earthly discipline, preparing him for that which lies ahead. In many cases it brings the sufferer into a state of mind in which he is not only ready but willing to

---

7. *The Southern Presbyterian Journal.* Jan. 1944.

leave this world. Through the atonement provided by
Christ the believer gains far more than he lost through the
fall in Adam, for in the incarnation human nature has
been, as it were, taken into the very bosom of Deity, and a
closer relationship established between God and man than
that which exists between God and the angels. Because of
this relationship man's life is ultimately made much richer
and fuller than was that of Adam before the fall, even his
physical body finally being transformed into the likeness
of Christ's glorious body. Paul says: "But we all, with
unveiled face, beholding as in a mirror the glory of the
Lord, are transformed into the same image from glory to
glory, even as from the Lord the Spirit," II Cor. 3:18. And
in I John 3:2 we read: "Beloved, now are we children of
God, and it is not yet made manifest what we shall be. We
know that, if he shall be made manifest, we shall be like
him; for we shall see him as he is."

On the other hand, death is never to be thought of as in
itself a blessing. Except as it is overruled for good in
Christ, it is an enemy, cruel, relentless, bringing grief and
misery in human hearts. It is a violent and unnatural rend-
ing apart of soul and body. It is something that under normal conditions should never have entered the world, and
that would not have been allowed except as it became
necessary as a punishment for sin. The Bible is uncompro-
misingly honest about death. It does not sentimentalize.
It informs us that death is the penalty for sin, and that its
infliction on the human race was an awful calamity. It
says, "The last enemy . . . . is death," I Cor. 15:26. When
the soul is torn away from the body, and all the tender affections and sweet associations are broken in a moment of
time, even the most godly cannot look forward to this mysterious change without a strange and uncanny feeling. The
soul without its body is incomplete.

This is the view presented in both the Old and the New
Testament. Many times the Old Testament saints cried out
to God against death. David spoke of the valley of the

shadow of death. Paul describes it as a terrible foe with
an awful sting like an adder. And again he said, "We ourselves groan within ourselves, waiting for our adoption, to
wit, the redemption of our body," Rom. 8:23. It is an enemy because it is the work of THE enemy, Satan. It is in
fact the fullest and climactic work of the enemy. It is an
alien invasion of God's creation by the power of evil, a
thing absolutely contrary to the nature of God. Christ
Himself, as He stood with the sorrowing relatives at the
grave of His friend Lazarus, wept as He saw the grief of
His friends and felt in His own soul a sense of the awful-
ness of this work of the great enemy. But there is a remedy, not of human but of Divine origin; for Christ has paid
the redemption price for His people, and now possesses the
power to overrule even this great calamity for their good.

While death, then, is no longer to be feared by the Christian it nevertheless remains a dreadful experience. Paul
expresses something of this when he likens the loss of the
body by the soul to a state of nakedness. In II Cor. 5:1-4 he
says: "For we know that if the earthly house of our tabernacle be dissolved, we have a building from God, a house
not made with hands, eternal, in the heavens. For verily
in this we groan, longing to be clothed upon with our habitation which is from heaven: if so be that being clothed we
shall not be found naked. For indeed we that are in this
tabernacle do groan, being burdened; not for that we would
be unclothed, but that we would be clothed upon, that what
is mortal may be swallowed up of life."

Here Paul expresses concern or a reticence about entering into the disembodied state. He seems to say that if we
could receive the resurrection body immediately, that is,
without an intervening disembodied state or a period of
soul nakedness as he expresses it, then the change would
certainly be welcome. It is at any rate clear that in his
teaching the physical body as well as the soul is an object
of redemption, and precious both to the Lord and to the
believer. There are some today who teach the heresy of the

resurrection of the soul only. But such a calamity seems
never to have entered the mind of Paul.

In verse eight of this same chapter Paul expresses himself as "willing rather to be absent from the body, and to
be at home with the Lord." In other words, we are taught
that while death is in itself an evil, yet the joy that comes
through entering into the presence of the Lord is so glorious and attractive that we should be willing and ready to
leave the body and to be present with the Lord whenever
the call comes.

Paul longs for relief from the burdens of life. As Dr.
Benjamin B. Warfield has expressed it, "The other world
is so glorious to him that he is not only willing but even
desires ('rather,' verse 8) to enter it even 'naked' — he is
well pleased to go abroad from the body and go home to
the Lord. Like Bunyan and the sweet singer, Paul, looking
beyond the confines of earth, can only say, 'Would God that
I were there!'

"This longing for relief from earthly life is repeated in
Romans (7:25), and the groaning expectation of the consummation as the swallowing up of corruption in incorruption is attributed in the wonderful words of Rom.
8:18ff. to the whole of the lower creation. All nature, says
Paul, travails in the same longing. And the consummation
brings not only relief to Christ's children, who have received the firstfruits of the Spirit, in the redemption of the
body, but also deliverance and renovation to all nature as
well."[8]

Paul further declares himself "in a strait betwixt the
two, having the desire to depart and be with Christ; for it
is very far better: yet," says he, "to abide in the flesh is
more needful for your sake," Phil. 1:23,24. In accordance
with this our attitude toward death should be that as long
as we are given health and strength we are willing and
even desire to remain in this life and accomplish as much

---

8. *Biblical And Theological Studies*, p. 490

as possible for the advancement of the kingdom and for our own growth in grace, but that when our time comes we go willingly and gladly. A faithful soldier at his post of duty resists all attempts to persuade him to leave until his task is accomplished. But when his duty has been performed and he receives orders to return he obeys gladly. "I am not tired of my work," wrote Adoniram Judson, the great Baptist missionary to Burma, "neither am I tired of the world; yet when Christ calls me home I shall go with the gladness of a school boy bounding away from school. Death will never take me by surprise; I am too strong in Christ."

Here we are reminded of an event reported concerning John Quincy Adams. It is said that one day in his eightieth year as he walked slowly along a Boston street he was accosted by a friend who said, "And how is John Quincy Adams today?" The former president of the United States replied graciously, "Thank you, John Quincy Adams is well, sir, quite well, I thank you. But the house in which he lives at present is becoming dilapidated. It is tottering upon the foundations. Time and the seasons have nearly destroyed it. Its roof is pretty well worn out, its walls are shattered, and it trembles with every wind. The old tenement is becoming almost uninhabitable, and I think John Quincy Adams will have to move out of it soon; but he himself is quite well, sir, quite well." And with that the venerable statesman, leaning heavily upon his cane, continued his slow walk down the street.

Another illustration of what death should mean to the Christian:

"I am standing upon the seashore. A ship at my side spreads her white sails to the morning breeze and starts for the blue ocean. She is an object of beauty and strength, and I stand and watch her until at length she hangs like a speck of white cloud just where the sea and sky come down to meet each other. Then someone at my side says, 'There, she is gone.' Gone where? Gone from my sight, that is all.

She is just as large in mast and hull and spar as she was when she left my side, and just as able to bear her load of living weights to its place of destination. Her diminished size is in me, not in her; and just at the moment when someone at my side says, 'There, she is gone,' on that distant shore there are other eyes watching for her coming and other voices ready to take up the glad shout, 'Here she comes' — and such is dying."[9]

Indeed, if we are Christians why should we be afraid of death? Why should we fear to meet our Saviour who has done more for us and who loves us more than any one else in the world, and to enter into a higher form of life and service? Unfortunately, even casual conversation with mourners at the time of death in a family reveals that many professedly Christian people do have such a fear, and that they have only the vaguest ideas about the state of the dead and the future life. But it is not intended that we should be afraid. We have been given a special promise to take care of that fear: "Yea, though I walk through the valley of the shadow of death, I will fear no evil; for thou art with me, thy rod and thy staff, they comfort me." Death is in reality only a translation from one phase of life to another. Far from marking the end, it marks the beginning of a fuller and more wonderful life than can ever be known on this earth. But while we may be afraid of death now, the experience of others has shown that when the end comes if we are Christians we will not be afraid.

"Our citizenship is in heaven," Phil. 3:20. Heaven is our home. Life in this world is only the preparatory school, the staging ground, as it were, to get us ready for the much greater life that lies ahead. God does not want us to become satisfied with life in this world. To that end He sends an appropriate amount of sorrow, suffering and disappointment to each of His children, in order that their antic-

---

9. *Source unknown.*

ipation of and appreciation for the heavenly life may be
the greater.

6. Comments by John Calvin

John Calvin had much to say about the attitude that the
Christian should have toward this life, present possessions,
and death, as viewed in the light of Scripture, and his com-
ments are worth quoting at length. He says:

"With whatever kind of tribulation we may be afflicted,
we should always keep this end in view — to habituate ourselves to a contempt of the present life, that we may thereby be excited to meditation on that which is to come. For
the Lord, knowing our strong natural inclination to a brut-
ish love of the world, adopts a most excellent method to re-
claim us and rouse us from our insensibility, that we may
not be too tenaciously attached to that foolish affection . . . .
Our mental eyes, dazzled with the vain splendor of riches,
power, and honors, cannot see to any considerable dis-
tance . . . . The whole soul, fascinated by carnal allurements,
seeks its felicity on earth. To oppose this evil, the Lord, by
continual lessons of misery, teaches His children the van-
ity of the present life. That they may not promise themselves profound and secure peace in it, he permits them to
be frequently disquieted and infested with wars and tu-
mults, with robberies and other injuries. That they may
not aspire with too much avidity after transient and uncertain riches, or depend on those which they possess, —
sometimes by exile, sometimes by the sterility of the land,
sometimes by conflagration, sometimes by other means, He
reduces them to indigence, or at least confines them within
the limits of mediocrity. That they may not be too com-
placently delighted with conjugal blessings, He either
causes them to be distressed with the wickedness of their
wives, or humbles them with a wicked offspring, or afflicts
them with want or loss of children. But if in all these things
He is more indulgent to them, yet that they may not be
inflated with vain glory, or improper confidence, He shows

them by disease and dangers the unstable and transitory
nature of all mortal blessings. We therefore truly derive
advantage from the discipline of the cross, only when we
learn that this life, considered in itself, is unquiet, turbu-
lent, miserable in numberless instances, and in no respect
altogether happy; and that all its reputed blessings are uncertain, transient, vain and adulterated with a mixture of
many evils; and in consequence of this at once conclude
that nothing can be sought or expected on earth but con-
flict, and that when we think of a crown we must raise our
eyes toward heaven. For it must be admitted, that the
mind is never seriously excited to desire and meditate on
the future life, without having previously imbibed a contempt for the present."

Calvin goes on to say, however, that the good things that
come to us in this world are of God's giving, and that we
must not be ungrateful for them. "But believers should ac-
custom themselves to such contempt of the present life, as
may not generate either hatred of life, or ingratitude
toward God. For this life, though it is replete with innu-
merable miseries, is yet deservedly reckoned among the
Divine blessings which must not be despised. Wherefore,
if we discover nothing of the Divine beneficence in it, we
are already guilty of no small ingratitude toward God Himself. But to believers especially it should be a testimony of
the Divine benevolence, since the whole of it is destined to
the advancement of their salvation. For before He dis-
covers to us the inheritance of eternal glory, He intends to
reveal Himself as our Father in inferior instances; and
those are the benefits which He daily confers upon us. . . .
And it is a far superior reason for gratitude, if we consider
that here we are in some measure prepared for the glory
of the heavenly kingdom. For the Lord has ordained, that
they who are to be hereafter crowned in heaven, must first
engage in conflicts on earth, that they may not triumph
without having surmounted the difficulties of warfare and
obtained the victory. . . .

"It belongs to the Lord to determine what shall conduce most to His glory. Therefore, if it becomes us 'to live and to die unto the Lord' (Rom. 14:7,8), let us leave the limits of our life and death to His decision; yet in such a manner, as ardently to desire and continually to meditate on the latter, but to despise the former in comparison with future immortality, and on account of the servitude of sin, to wish to forsake it whenever it shall please the Lord.

"But it is monstrous, that instead of this desire of death, multitudes who boast themselves to be Christians, are filled with such a dread of it, that they tremble whenever it is mentioned, as if it were the greatest calamity that could befall them. It is no wonder, indeed, if our natural feelings should be alarmed at hearing of our dissolution. But it is intolerable that there should not be in a Christian breast sufficient light of piety to overcome and suppress all that fear with superior consolation. For if we consider, that this unstable, depraved, corruptible, frail, withering tabernacle of our body is dissolved, in order that it may hereafter be restored to a durable, perfect, incorruptible, and heavenly glory, — will not faith constrain us ardently to desire what nature dreads? If we recall that by death we are recalled from exile to inhabit our own country, and that a heavenly one, shall we derive thence no consolation? . . . . This we may positively conclude, that *no man has made any good proficiency in the school of Christ, but he who joyfully expects both the day of death and that of the final resurrection.* . . . [Ital. mine, L. B.] 'Look up,' saith the Lord, 'and lift up your heads; for your redemption draweth nigh' (Luke 21:28) . . . . Let us therefore acquire a sounder judgment; and notwithstanding the opposition of the blind and stupid cupidity of our flesh, let us not hesitate ardently to desire the advent of the Lord, as of all events the most auspicious. For he shall come to us as a Redeemer, to deliver us from this bottomless gulf of evils and miseries, and to introduce us into that blessed inheritance of His life and glory.[10]

7. Every Person's Life a Completed Plan

It often seems to us that a person is taken from this life before his work is finished. Particularly is this true when a father or mother is taken from a family, or when a promising young person, or a much needed Christian leader or official dies. From the human viewpoint no life ever seemed so unfinished as did that of Jesus when at the early age of thirty-three He met death by crucifixion. How desperately the world needed His continued teaching and preaching and His miracles of healing! How desperately His influence would be needed in the new Church! But His *real* work was not that which human minds thought it to be. The night before He was killed He said, "I have glorified thee on the earth, having accomplished the work which Thou hast given me to do," John 17:4. As He hung on the cross, dying for the sins of others, He said, "It is finished." From the human viewpoint it looked as though His ministry had just begun. But from the Divine viewpoint He had accomplished that which He came to do. The human viewpoint saw only the external side of His work which related to the people immediately around Him. But from the Divine viewpoint He had accomplished the redemption of His people, which was His real work.

From the human viewpoint how desperately the continued preaching and guidance of Paul was needed in the new churches! But he, speaking by inspiration, could say, "I have finished the course." And how they needed Stephen, and James, in the early Church! We would have said, "Unfinished," But God said, "Finished." And how often today when a young father or mother or boy or girl is taken we cry out, "Unfinished." But God says, "Finished."

---

10. *Institutes*, Bk. III: Ch. ix; Sec. i-v.

Clearly, accomplishment in life cannot be measured in terms of years alone. It often happens that those who die young have accomplished more than others who live to old age. Even infants, who sometimes have been with their parents only a few days, or even hours, may leave profound influences that change the entire course of the life of the family. And undoubtedly, from the Divine viewpoint, the specific purpose for which they were sent into the world was accomplished. It is our right neither to take life prematurely, nor to insist on its extension beyond the mark that God has set for it.

Some speak of the "problem" of death. For the Christian there should be no more a problem of death than there is a problem of faded flowers or of a clouded sky. God has made this so clear in His word that there can be no grounds to question it. It is only when we fail to think soberly about life that we have the feeling that it should be all sunshine. Undoubtedly death has been for many the one way of release from burdens and pains that had become too great to be borne, as with the hopelessly incurable, and the aged. For others it has meant escape from suffering or disappointment that would have come to them in later life. As this world is constituted there must be shadows as well as light, night as well as day, pain as well as pleasure, a departure from life as well as an entrance into it. That richer life, which is the soul's true destiny, can be attained only by passing through the portals of death.

A further point worthy of notice is this: — There seems to be a widespread belief even among evangelical Christians that to die before the coming of Christ is a misfortune, and that it would be a special blessing to be a member of that last generation which shall be on earth and which shall be translated at the Lord's coming. That there should be a natural shrinking from death at all times is understandable. But the fact is that those who die in the Lord have the inexpressibly high privilege of living and sharing with Christ in the Messianic Kingdom. Surely that is a most valuable experience which will not be the privilege of those who are alive and who are raptured at His coming. In this sense we may distinguish between (1) the Messianic Kingdom, or the Kingdom of Christ, which relates to time, and (2) the eternal Kingdom which follows those events.

8. Making Preparation for Death

How would you want to spend the time if you knew that tomorrow would be your last day on earth? Would you need to spend it asking for that forgiveness of sin which you should have asked for long ago? It is, of course, infinitely better to make a death-bed repentance than not to repent at all. But many who put off until the last moment the matter of getting right with God find themselves unable to repent at that time. A wise counsellor, Dr. Charles Hodge, once said: "It is important that when we come to die we have nothing to do but to die." Such a one can wait calmly the coming of death, knowing that his sins are forgiven and that all will be well.

John Wesley was once asked, "If you knew that you would die at twelve o'clock tomorrow night, how would you spend the intervening time?" "Why," was the answer, "just as I intend to spend it. I would preach tonight at Gloucester and again tomorrow morning. After that I would ride to Tewkesbury, preach in the afternoon and meet the society in the evening. I should then repair to friend Martin's house, as he expects me; converse, pray with the family, retire to my room at ten o'clock, commend myself to my Heavenly Father, lie down to sleep and wake up in glory."

The fact that the young as well as the old, and that the righteous as well as sinners, die, should make every one aware that his own time is very uncertain. The Christian should be ready for his Lord's coming at any time. "Therefore be ye also ready; for in an hour that ye think not the

Son of man cometh," Matt. 24:44. In the parable of the Ten Virgins, five made preparation and were ready; five neglected to prepare and were not ready. "And . . . the bridegroom came: and they that were ready went in with him to the marriage feast: and the door was shut. Afterward came also the other virgins, saying, Lord, Lord, open to us. But he answered and said, Verily I say unto you, I know you not. Watch therefore, for ye know not the day nor the hour," Matt. 25:10-13.

Reports come from various sources concerning the manner in which the righteous and the wicked die. Many approach that infinitely important event without any adequate realization of its meaning, and many are in such a physical state that they cannot think clearly in their last moments. But those who have taken a stand either for or against Christ often reflect that attitude as the soul takes its departure. For the Christian death should come as quietly as the twilight hour with its cool peace and its embracing rest. "Let me die the death of the righteous, And let my last end be like his," Nu. 23:10. For those outside of Christ death is a terrible thing. Their fears are fully justified. For them it means, "after death the judgment." With nothing more substantial than the speculations of philosophers and naturalists or the musings of poets and novelists, they are utterly unprepared to face the future. These are the lost. What emotions other than terror can possibly possess a person when he finally is given an insight into the ultimate reality of things and who with his sins unforgiven goes out into a Christless eternity?

We sometimes hear it said that death through cancer, tuberculosis, or some other disease in which the person may be sick and perhaps suffer for a period of time is a horrible way to die. We believe, however, that for most people such a death, rather than one that occurs suddenly, as in heart failure, drowning or accident, at least affords a final period of preparation both as regards the person's spiritual well-

being and his earthly affairs. This, too, is true of those
who attain to advanced years. As one has said,

> " 't is meet that we should pause a while,
>   Ere we put off this mortal coil,
>   And in the stillness of old age,
>   Muse on our earthly pilgrimage."

One of the most painful thoughts about death is that of
having to leave behind so much that we value or hold dear,
— positions we have attained, earthly possessions, past accomplishments, unfinished projects, etc. But Rev. 14:13,
after pronouncing blessed those who die in the Lord, and
declaring that they rest from their labors, says: "For their
works follow with them." That means that every good
work that we have done will go with us and will be our possession over there. Even our material possessions, while
they cannot be taken with us, can be sent on ahead, — if
invested wisely in the Lord's work, exchanging earthly
values for heavenly values. "Lay not up for yourselves
treasures upon the earth, where moth and rust consume,
and where thieves break through and steal: but lay up for
yourselves treasures in heaven, where neither moth nor
rust doth consume, and where thieves do not break through
nor steal," Matt. 6:19,20. That assures permanent possession. In the light of Scripture teaching, the only money
that we really have is that which we have wisely given
away. That is the way, and in fact it is the only way, in
which we can take our possessions with us. Christ admon-
ishes us to do that. Christian giving and Christian spend-
ing involve a real test of faith.

Most people are reluctant to give serious consideration
to the reality of death until it is forced upon them. This,
however, is not the part of wisdom. The Bible frequently
confronts us with the fact of death. We read there of the
careers of many and great men. But no matter how long
they lived, the repeated comment is, "And he died."

Sooner or later death is sure to come in the experience of each of us. When it does come the most sensible course is to meet it squarely. Unfortunately, in some homes children receive no proper teaching concerning its meaning. The subject is scarcely mentioned, and the children may even be forbidden to attend funerals. But some day those children, perhaps alone and without warning, will be forced to stand by the death-bed of mother, father, brother or sister, or perhaps face it on the battlefield in its cruelest form. What then will be their reaction? Nothing is more certain than the fact of death; nothing is more uncertain than the time at which it will come.

Surely it is the part of wisdom to be prepared for this certain attack. Modern psychology is showing that the most effective way to deal with a situation that causes intense distress or grief is not to suppress it or drive it down into our subconscious mind where it continues to harass and upset us, but to meet it openly, discuss it with others, and, so far as possible, seek to understand it. If we try to suppress it or ignore it much damage may be done to our minds, bodies and souls. A recent article, "The Death We Face," by Dr. John R. Richardson, illustrates this point quite clearly. Says he:

"Dr. John G. MacKenzie, professor of Psychology in Paton College, Nottingham, England, in his book, *Souls in the Making,* told of a family in England which had lost a beloved son in the first World War. These parents were distracted with grief and as the days and months passed the mother settled down into an unrelieved depression. This melancholic state threatened her mental balance until at last MacKenzie was consulted. He inquired of the father whether they ever talked about the son. 'No,' the father told him, 'that is the one thing we do not talk about.' He stated that they left this topic out of their conversations and tried to keep it out of their thoughts. Then Dr. MacKenzie told the father that the family was pursuing exactly the wrong course. He made him promise that instead of refraining from conversation about the son they would talk freely about him. What do you suppose was the result? Dr. MacKenzie affirmed that there was a complete cure of the soul in this regard and a gradual restoration of happiness. This," adds Dr. Richardson, "is but one illustration of the danger of repressing the thought of death into the subconscious mind. When we drive it down into the subconscious regions of our personalities, it haunts us all our days, and as the New Testament states, through this fear of death we shall be all our lifetime subject to bondage. Instead of discussion about death being morbid, it is healthy and we should learn to talk freely and naturally about it in a healthy state of mind."[11]

9. What Happens at Death

The Scriptures represent death as primarily a separation of soul and body. "The dust returneth to the earth as it was, and the spirit returneth unto God who gave it," Eccl. 12:7. "For as the body apart from the spirit is dead, even so faith apart from works is dead," James 2:26. Death is a transition from one realm to another, and from one kind of life to another. For the Christian it means the cleansing of the soul from the last vestiges of sin and an entrance into the mansions of light. This is well expressed in the Westminster Shorter Catechism, where, in response to the question, "What benefits do believers receive from Christ at death?" (Q. 37), the answer is given: "The souls of believers are at their death made perfect in holiness, and do immediately pass into glory; and their bodies, being still united to Christ, do rest in their graves, till the resurrection."

Human life is a boundless adventure which is to continue on through all eternity. The present life is but the first stage of a long career. What we call death is not the end, but only the entrance of the soul into a new and more won-

---

11. *The Southern Presbyterian Journal.*

drous world. By its very nature this transition must be mysterious and awe-inspiring. To some people there is given in this life a long series of fascinating and thrilling adventures, involving perhaps many great accomplishments. But we may be sure that the first five minutes after death will bring experiences for the soul far more remarkable and awesome than anything that ever has been experienced in this world. Picture even faintly, if you can, those first moments in glory land. Undoubtedly the person first of all sees Christ his Saviour, the One by whose redemptive work he has been brought to salvation, and whose he is. And may we not believe that he also sees his Christian loved ones who have gone before and who now come to welcome him? We know that they are with Christ, for He Himself has said, "I go to prepare a place for you. And if I go and prepare a place for you, I come again, and will receive you unto myself; that where I am, there ye may be also," John 14:2,3. In the parable of the rich man and Lazarus we are told that the angels carried Lazarus to the place of rest. That would seem to indicate that a heavenly escort awaits the Lord's people at their death and leads them in triumph from earth to heaven. And this would seem further to be entirely appropriate since the Lord, by His redemptive work, is rescuing souls one by one from the kingdom of Satan and transferring them to the kingdom of heaven where they shall be forever associated with Himself and His people.

Also, we think of death as a home-going, and of heaven as our eternal home. In the Old Testament we have this description of death: "Man goeth to his everlasting home, and the mourners go about the streets," Eccl. 12:5. Paul says that we are "willing rather to be absent from the body, and to be at home with the Lord," II Cor. 5:8. The most distinctive feature about home is that it is where our loved ones are. It is a great privilege just to go home and renew the old family ties. Some of the happiest moments of our earthly lives have been those when we turned our faces toward home. Many of us no doubt have memories of those events that we can never forget.

We know but very little about what transpires on the other side of the grave, but of this much we may be sure, that suddenly, at the moment of death, all things appear in a new perspective. The one who is called exchanges comparative darkness and limited knowledge for new light and knowledge commensurate with his new estate, — "For now we see in a mirror darkly; but then face to face: now I know in part; but then shall I know fully even as also I was fully known," I Cor. 13:12. The things that the person thought important, — his business affairs, the season's crops, tomorrow's tasks, his success in pleasing those around him, — all of these no longer matter at all. All of earth's cares and problems suddenly are left behind. And in their place the things to which he perhaps had given but little attention stand out as all-important, — his attitude toward Christ, his Christian witness to those about him, his prayer life, the motives which underlay his public and private actions. He will then see that the important thing was not how much he did or how much he gave, but with what motives or with what purpose he acted. He will wonder, not how much of his money he should have given to the Lord, but why he withheld so much of the Lord's money for himself. He will see that no material possessions really belonged to him, but that all of the money and lands and other possessions really belonged to the Lord, and that he was only a steward to whom their management was entrusted temporarily.

Five minutes after he is in heaven he will be overwhelmed by truths that he had known all along but somehow had never fully grasped. He will wish with all his heart that he could recall just the one-hundredth part of the time that he let slip through his fingers, that he could recall the lost opportunities that presented themselves for the Lord's service and for better living, — that from the fields that were "white already unto harvest" (John 4:35) he had led many more souls to salvation. He will wish that he had gained a much fuller knowledge of divine truth as it is set forth in the Bible, for that is the knowledge that he will then live by; and he will wish that in his Bible study he had made a much fuller acquaintance with the Old Testament and New Testament saints in whose company he will find himself. Many will be saved no doubt "so as through fire," saved, but entering heaven practically bankrupt, their life's work, like wood, hay, stubble, having been burned up (I Cor. 3:12-15). There will loom up before him the endless possibilities of the heavenly life, and there will blossom forth within his own being (which was created in the image of God) a thousand new talents and powers all unsuspected, these to develop and grow and to be his possession for ever and ever.

10. Christians Not to Sorrow As Those Who Have No Hope

When a believing loved one is taken it ill becomes a Christian to give himself over to unrestrained grief, or to express resentment toward an act of divine providence. Such conduct does not commend the faith that we profess. It is but natural that at such a time we should be acutely conscious of an aching void. We know that we shall no longer experience the kind words of love and helpfulness from the departed one. The widow is left to mourn the loss of her husband as she tends her fatherless children; the parents miss the cheerfulness of youth when a son or daughter is taken. We sorrow over the loss of our friends. We would be less than human if we did not feel that loss. But we rejoice that they have gone to the heavenly home. The loss is ours, not theirs.

Weeping is not out of place at a Christian funeral. Jesus wept at the tomb of Lazarus. The Bible sanctions mourning and a respect for the bodies of those who have departed. Periods of mourning were authorized in Scripture, depending upon the character and station of the dead. But surely the black clothing, the long veil and such dismal signs of mourning as once were the general custom are entirely out of place. It often happens that our funerals are too black, and that we act as though we had but very little faith. We should always remember that we bury only the body, not the soul, of our loved one, that the soul has gone to be with the Lord.

Nowhere more than at a Christian funeral should the world see the blessings of faith. At that particular time when hearts are more receptive than usual a special opportunity is presented to witness to the saving power of Christ and to point others to Him. The Christian doctrines concerning the immortality of the soul, God's redemptive love for His people, and the certainty of future rewards and punishments probably can be more effectively presented at that time than at any other.

We are told that in the early days of the Church the pagans were often amazed at the calmness of the Christians in the hour of death. There was something about their noble and fearless bearing that pagan philosophy could not explain. That attitude seemed strange then, and still does, to the man of the world, for he cannot understand how it is possible for anyone to view death mildly and calmly. Christians who have been enlightened from the Bible concerning death and spiritual things do not fear death. But it is unfortunately true that many faithful saints have not received much instruction on this subject, or at least have failed to grasp its full meaning, and that they still share with the world the fear of death. It should be our duty to help them toward a fuller understanding of this truth, that they may come to possess the spiritual peace that is rightfully theirs.

That this is the teaching set forth in Scripture is clear enough. Writing to the Thessalonians Paul said: "But we would not have you ignorant, brethren, concerning them that fall asleep; that ye sorrow not, even as the rest, who have no hope," I Thess. 4:13. In preparing the disciples for His own death Jesus said, "Let not your heart be troubled, neither let it be fearful," John 14:27. And again, "If ye loved me, ye would have rejoiced, because I go unto the Father," John 14:28. The disciples did not rejoice, because of their incomplete understanding of what was involved; nor is it easy for us to rejoice when a loved one is taken from us, even though we know that he is saved. But certainly the Apostle John when, in apocalyptic vision, he saw a great multitude that no man could number, standing before the throne, clothed with white robes, bathed in the dazzling splendor of light inaccessible, and heard them cry with a loud voice, "Salvation unto our God who sitteth upon the throne, and unto the Lamb" (Rev. 7:10), could not have grieved when he knew that his loved ones were there.

To show resentment at such times is to sin against God. It is in effect a challenge to His providential control. It means further that we are cutting ourselves off so that we have to bear our grief alone. Such actions create a great gulf between God and ourselves. Nor are we deliberately to run away from grief and seek to lose ourselves in an orgy of senseless activity. That is like taking an opiate to relieve pain, affording at best only temporary relief, and in the long run leaving us in a worse state than before. The only way for a Christian to meet sorrow is to meet it as his Master did, calmly and courageously, with implicit faith that whatever our Father in heaven does is right, — "Not my will, but thine be done." The glorious thing about this is that even the weakest and most ignorant among us can have this faith if he will but keep open the channel of communication between himself and his heavenly Father.

When our loved ones are called and we are left behind, that means that God still has work for us to do. Whether that work be in behalf of others or in the further development of our own spiritual nature, He expects us to adjust to the new situation and to do that which needs to be done. We have His promise of sufficient help: "And as thy days, so shall thy strength be," Deut. 33:25. As we busy our-

selves in the tasks at hand new interests are developed and
perhaps a whole new field of service is opened up. It is
well to remember, too, that time is a great healer, and that
as the days come and go and we are further removed from
the event, the sense of loss, while still very real, becomes
much less painful.

Though from our own viewpoint the loss of a loved one
seems to be a tragedy, we know that for him this has been
his coronation day. We know that ere long we too shall
pass through that same portal. Except for the sense of
personal loss we should rejoice when that supreme blessedness comes to a loved one, and be willing to bear the loneliness and separation for his or her sake, as a mother does
when her daughter marries and goes far away to the happiness of her own home. Too often our thoughts are only
about ourselves, and our tears flow only because of selfish
motives which we feel may now be frustrated. If we were
really thinking of the welfare of our friend we would wear
a beaming countenance and rejoice at his promotion to the
heavenly kingdom. The best description of this change still
is found in Paul's words, "Absent from the body . . . at
home with the Lord," II Cor. 5:8.

Furthermore, those who have passed on undoubtedly
would not want to come back to this world, with all of its
sin and suffering, its injustice and limitations, even if that
were possible. To return to this world after experiencing
even briefly the heavenly life would be as inappropriate
as for a college graduate to go back and enroll again in the
first grade, or for one who has become President of the
United States to resign that high office and hire himself
out as a factory worker or farm hand for such work as he
may have done in his early years. If our vision could pen-
etrate the veil that separates this world from the next, so
that we could really comprehend the beauty and glory of
that realm, we may be sure that we would be far less given
to tears, that we would indeed rejoice greatly when our

loved ones are called home. Christians sad and sorrowing in this world are like

> "New-born princes crying in their cradles,
> Not knowing that kingdoms await them."

The present writer has found the following illustration quite helpful in class work to show what our attitude should be toward the departure of loved ones. Suppose a relative or friend is given a trip around the world with all expenses paid, all hotel accommodations and sight-seeing tours arranged, and in association with a very desirable group of friends. Suppose the trip includes a tour of our Rocky mountain and Pacific coast states, a luxury liner or airplane across the Pacific to Hawaii, Japan, Australia, India, Egypt, Palestine, Greece, Italy, Switzerland, Germany, France, England, and back across the Atlantic. Such a trip would be considered a great privilege. It would mean temporary separation, but we would be happy that our friend should have such a privilege, and we would look forward to seeing him after the trip was over. The experience of death is somewhat like that, — the breaking of personal ties, temporary separation, then permanent reunion in that better land. Even in this world when friends come together after years of separation, the intervening time seems to fade away as if there had been no separation at all.

Furthermore, in time of bereavement we find great comfort in our belief that God's providential control extends over all these things, even the sinful acts of evil man being foreseen, permitted and overruled for a greater good. Our limited vision oftentimes does not permit us to understand why certain things happen. But undoubtedly if we could see all events from the divine viewpoint and understood God's purpose in bringing them to pass, we would see that every event has its appointed place in that plan as a whole, and that it is designed for our good. We have Paul's statement to that effect: "We know that to them that love God all things work together for good, even to them that are called according to his purpose," Rom. 8:28. We readily grant that it often does not look that way now. From our viewpoint it often looks as though there was much more to be accomplished before the person's life course would be complete. But undoubtedly from the divine viewpoint the work appointed for each individual is completed before he is called.

Some years ago Dr. Clarence E. Macartney expressed this very clearly when in speaking of God's providential control of all events he said: "The misfortunes and adversities of life, so called, assume a different color when we look at them through this glass. It is sad to hear people trying to live over their lives again and saying to themselves: 'If I had chosen a different profession,' 'If I had taken a different turning of the road,' 'If I had married another person.' All of this is weak and unChristian. The web of destiny we have woven, in a sense, with our hands, and yet God has had His part in it. It is God's part in it, and not ours, that gives us faith and hope."

And to the same effect Blaise Pascal, a celebrated French mathematician and writer, in a wonderful letter to a bereaved friend, instead of repeating the ordinary platitudes of consolation, comforted him with this doctrine, saying: "If we regard this event, not as the effect of chance, not as a fatal necessity of nature, but as a result inevitable, just, holy, of a decree of His providence, conceived from all eternity, to be executed in such a year, day, hour, and in such a place and manner, we shall adore in humble silence the impenetrable loftiness of His secrets; we shall venerate the sanctity of His decrees; we shall bless the act of His providence; and uniting our will with that of God Himself, we shall wish with Him, in Him and for Him, the thing that He has willed in us and for us from all eternity."

11. Prayers for the Dead

We believe that it avails nothing to pray for the dead. That practice is followed in the Roman Catholic Church, where it is closely connected with, and is a logical consequence of, their doctrine of purgatory. The high Anglican Church, which holds a position about half way between the Roman Catholic and the representative Protestant churches, also follows that custom. But practically all other Protestant churches reject it.

Prayers for the dead imply that their state has not yet been fixed, and that it can be improved at our request. We hold, however, that there is no change of character or of destiny after death, that what the person is at death he remains throughout all eternity. We find an abundance of Scripture teaching to the effect that this world only is the place of opportunity for salvation, and that when this probation or testing period is past only the assignment of rewards and punishments remain. Consequently we hold that all prayers, baptisms, masses, or other rituals of whatever kind for the dead are superfluous, vain and unscriptural.

As for the righteous dead, they are in the immediate presence of Christ, in a perfect environment of holiness and beauty and glory where their every need is satisfied. They have no need of any petitions from us. They lack nothing that our prayers can satisfy. Their state is as perfect as it can be until the day when they and we receive our resurrection bodies. To petition God to change the status or condition of His loved ones in glory, or to suggest that He is not doing enough for them, is, to say the least, highly presumptuous, even though it may be well intended.

As for the wicked dead, their state too is fixed and irrevocable. They have had their opportunity. They have sinned away their day of grace. The uplifting and restraining influence of the Holy Spirit as directed towards them has been withdrawn. It is understandable that remaining relatives and friends should be concerned about them. But the determination of their status after death is the prerogative of God alone. The holiness and justice of God are all-sufficient guarantees that while some by His grace will be rewarded far above their deserts, none will be punished beyond their deserts.

It is very significant that in Scripture we have not one single instance of prayer for the dead, nor any admonition to that end. In view of the many admonitions for prayer for those in this world, even admonitions to pray for our enemies, the silence of Scripture regarding prayer for the dead would seem to be inexplainable if it availed anything.

12. Burial or Cremation?

What is the right method for disposal of the body? In the final analysis it is no doubt correct to say that the manner of disposal is not a matter of vital importance. We do not believe, for instance, that in the resurrection there will be any difference between those who are buried in the graves of the earth and those whose bodies were destroyed by fire, or devoured by wild beasts, or drowned in the sea, or blown to bits by the explosion of bombs. Certainly the martyrs who were burned for the faith and whose ashes were scattered by the winds shall arise in the resurrection, and their bodies shall be not one whit less glorious than those of others who received burial. There is no limit to the power of God. He who in the first place made the body from the elements of the earth can bring again the body that has been distintegrated by whatever means. The identical particles are not essential to a resurrection. A sailor buried at sea rises as surely as if he had been expensively embalmed and buried in the family plot.

But this does not mean that there is not a great difference between burial and cremation. Certainly under normal conditions we show much more respect for the bodies of our loved ones if they are tenderly laid away in the earth, under the coverlet of green, in the posture of rest or sleep, and in as good a state of preservation as possible. The body is as really and eternally a part of man as is his spirit, and the resurrection of the body is an indispensable part of his salvation.

We cannot bring ourselves deliberately to take the body of a dear one, only less precious than the soul that it enshrined, and give it to the flames for violent destruction, even though we know that the spirit has departed. If we attach a sentimental value to a Bible or an article of clothing or other keepsake, how much more should we treat reverently the body that has been so much more intimately associated with the person. No matter with what refinements cremation is carried out, it still carries with it the idea of violence and destruction.

In the Bible fire is the type or symbol of destruction, complete and without remedy, the condemnation due for sin. In the sacrificial offering the animal was regarded as bearing the sins of the person, as being under condemnation, and therefore it was consumed upon the altar. In a few cases the bodies of criminals were burnt, to indicate the greatness of their sin and the severity of their punishment. After Achan had brought defeat upon Israel by taking "the accursed thing" that God had forbidden, we read: "And Joshua said, Why hast thou troubled us? Jehovah shall trouble thee this day. And all Israel stoned him with stones, and they burned them with fire, and stoned them with stones. And they raised over him a great heap of stones unto this day," Joshua 7:25,26.

Another case somewhat similar is that of King Saul. After he had disobeyed God, he was defeated in battle by the Philistines and died a shameful death that was practically suicide. His three sons died with him, and the armies of Israel fled. The Philistines cut off the head of the king, hung his armor in their heathen temple, and "fastened his body to the wall of Bethshan." We read that "when the inhabitants of Jabesh-gilead heard concerning him that which the Philistines had done to Saul, all the valiant men arose, and went all night, and took the body of Saul and the bodies of his sons from the wall of Bethshan; and they came to Jabesh, and burnt them there. And they took their bones, and buried them under the tamarisk tree in Jabesh, and fasted seven days," I Sam. 31:10-13.

The narrative shows that the procedure followed in regard to Saul was an abnormal and desperate measure. One Bible commentary says: "This was not a Hebrew custom. It was probably resorted to on this occasion to prevent all risk of further insult . . . . Burial was the usual Hebrew mode of disposal of their dead," (Jamieson, Fausset and Brown).

The example of the method that God Himself followed in disposing of the body of Moses should be noted. We read that when "Moses the servant of Jehovah died there in the land of Moab," that "he (God) buried him in the valley in the land of Moab over against Bethpeor; but no man knoweth of his sepulchre unto this day," Deut. 34:5,6. God's method was burial, not cremation.

Abraham purchased a cave in which to lay his beloved Sarah. Jacob buried Leah and Rachel. Abraham, Isaac, Jacob, Joseph, David, Solomon, etc., were buried.

In the New Testament the same teaching is continued. We have particularly the example of Jesus, whose body was reverently embalmed with precious spices, wrapped in a clean linen cloth, and tenderly laid in a tomb. Surely the divine precedent in the burial, not the burning, of His body should be the authoritative example for all Christians. Christians need no other reason for burial than that. The body of John the Baptist was buried, as were also those of all the other New Testament saints whose records are given.

Cremation was thus not the practice of the saints of God in either the Old Testament or the New. Rather it was of heathen origin. The early Christians followed the Jewish custom of burying the dead, and repudiated cremation, which was customary in the time of the early Roman Empire. The church historian, Philip Schaff, writes, "The primitive Christians always showed tender care for the dead, under a vivid impression of the unbroken communion of the saints and the future resurrection of the body in glory. For Christianity redeems the body as well as the soul and consecrates it a temple of the Holy Spirit. Hence the Greek and Roman custom of burning the corpse (crematio) was repugnant to Christian feeling and sacredness of the body."

Dr. Wm. C. Robinson, of Columbia Theological Seminary, writing on this subject says: "Following the Jewish custom, the Christians washed the bodies of the dead, wrapped them in linen cloths, sometimes embalmed them, and then, in the presence of ministers, relatives and friends, with prayer and the singing of psalms, committed their deceased bodies as seeds of the resurrection bodies to the bosom of the earth. Generally those burials were in sepulchral chambers with square-cornered recesses (loculi) in the walls as burial places. The corpse was wound in wrappings, without coffin, and the openings were closed with tiles of brick and marble. The Christian catacombs, as visible witness to the hope of the resurrection, carried their weight with the Roman people. Indeed, even Julian the Apostate traced the rapid spread and power of Christianity to three causes: benevolence, care of the dead, and honesty.

"The Christian custom was sustained by several texts from First and Second Corinthians. In opposing fornication, the Apostle wrote: 'Know ye not that your body is a temple of the Holy Spirit, which is in you which ye have from God? and ye are not your own; for ye were brought with a price: glorify God therefore in your body.' In opposing inter-marriage with unbelievers he reminds the Christians: 'What agreement hath a temple of God with idols? for ye are a temple of the living God.' In warning against dividing the congregation, he says: 'Know ye not

that ye are a temple of God, and that the Spirit of God
dwelleth in you? If any man destroyeth the temple of God,
him shall God destroy; for the temple of God is holy, and
such are ye.' In the great resurrection chapter he finds an
analogy between our sowing seed and having them sprout
into a living body and our looking for its resurrection in
incorruption — glory — power — a *spiritual* body."

Dr. Robinson then draws this conclusion: "Brethren,
weigh these texts, before you exchange the Christian custom of burying or entombing the bodies that are temples
of the Holy Ghost for a custom which primitive Christianity universally rejected. The graves of the saints are sanctified by Christ's rest in the tomb; and the bodies of believers being still united to Christ do rest in their graves
until the resurrection."[12]

We can only conclude that the practice of cremation,
which in our day seems to be becoming more common particularly in the larger city mortuaries, is anti-Christian
and should have no place in the practice of the believer. It
has no support in Scripture. The early Church rejected it
as a heathen custom, as dishonoring to the body, and as sug-
gesting the denial of the resurrection. Most of those who
advocate it in our day are religious liberals or humanists
who have little or no faith in the literal resurrection of
the body, and not a few of them have either discarded
Christianity or never gave serious allegiance to it in the
first place.

Strange as it may seem, the passages in the Bible that
are appealed to by advocates of cremation are those concerning Achan and Saul. But surely these two incidents
do not commend cremation as a reverent and desirable
means of disposing of the body of a loved one. Rather
they militate against such practice. But so anxious are the
advocates of cremation to find some Scripture support that
will appeal to Christians that in the absence of any others
they resort even to these.

---

12. *The Southern Presbyterian Journal*, July 30, 1952.

It need only to be said further that in regard to funerals Christians should avoid the ostentatious show so often seen in modern funerals, and should spend only a modest amount that will in nowise impoverish those who remain behind. It is rather noticeable that as a general rule people tend to have elaborate funerals in inverse proportion to the amount of true religion that they have. True Christians will not attempt to emulate the world, which sees in the funeral service only the end of an earthly life, but in full recognition of the Biblical truths concerning death and the future life will seek to give proper respect to the bodies of their loved ones and at the same time to center the attention of those present on the reality of the future life.

Immortality

II. Immortality

1. The Doctrine Stated

"If a man die, shall he live again?" Job 14:14.

For the Christian the answer to that question is found in the words of Jesus:

"I am the resurrection, and the life: he that believeth on me, though he die, yet shall he live; and whosoever liveth and believeth on me shall never die," John 11:25,26.

There is scarcely any other subject of religious thought that holds so keen and such a universal interest for us as that of the future life. It has exercised the mind of man in every age, and invariably there has been an innate longing in the hearts of individuals to perpetuate themselves beyond the grave. It is, therefore, not merely an academic question, but one that presses for an answer at the door of each one of us. Ultimately it will be the supreme question for each of us. It is a question aroused primarily not by fear of the future, but by a natural God-given desire to enter into that larger life and destiny which we instinctively feel is ahead.

The term that we generally use to designate the life of which we are speaking is *immortality*. Precisely what, then do we understand by that term? In its fullest sense,

Immortality means the eternal, continuous, conscious existence of the soul after the death of the body.

That we shall live again is surely no more wonderful or mysterious than that we are alive now. The real wonder rather would seem to be that after having not been in existence through an eternity that is past we now are in ex-

istence. Surely it is far more incredible that from not having been, we are, than that from actual being we shall continue to be. Nor is it any more wonderful that as human
beings we shall continue to live in a renewed body than it
is that life on this earth is now perpetuated from generation to generation by means of a body. We are familiar
with the latter and tend to think of it as natural, routine
and commonplace; but that does not make it any the less
mysterious.

The doctrine of immortality does not in itself tell us anything about the resurrection body, or whether, indeed,
there shall be a resurrection body. Christians believe, of
course, not only that the soul continues to exist, but that
eventually there is to be a resurrection of the body, so that
they shall be restored to the condition normal for human
beings.

As we stand looking into that dark corridor which sooner or later all must enter we ask with Job, "If a man die,
shall he live again?" At every funeral we instinctively
wonder, What has happened to that friend who has died?
Where is he now? The natural instincts of our nature tell
us that we shall live again, and the great majority of men
have always believed in a future life.

History shows that man has an instinctive longing for
immortality. The ancient religions and mythologies and
all forms of true and false religions in our day are the expressions and developments of this conviction. The belief
in immortality has taken many different forms among the
races of mankind, and has assumed various degrees of
strength and dignity. Sometimes it has been little more
than a shadowy hope, a vague feeling or an indefinite yearn-
ing, with the basic idea that eventually good will be rewarded and evil punished. But in some form or other it has
been held by every tribe and nation.

That the belief in immortality holds a prominent place
in the thinking of our day is shown by the vast number of
books, magazines, articles, etc., which deal with this sub-

ject in one form or another. It seems that instead of out-growing this belief, the race as it develops grows more strongly into it. This is all the more remarkable when we consider that there is much to militate against it. The inevitableness of death, for instance, would of itself seem to lead to a despair of the hereafter. Those who are living sinful lives would gladly escape a hereafter in which they are to be brought to judgment. They would in fact readily accept annihilation. Many who experience an undue pro-portion of the miseries of this world would avoid another if possible. It must be admitted that if the prospect of a future existence be not illuminated by the light of the Gos-pel there is little in it to make it appear attractive and much in it to make one apprehensive if not indeed fright-ened. Added to this is the fact that no one can give positive proof of a future life, and that even Christian believers at times have had doubts. Yet the race continues to be-lieve in immortality.

2. Immortality in the Ancient Religions

The religion of ancient Babylon and Assyria, as found in the old Accadian literature, contains many hymns, some of them penitential like the Psalms. Some of these are as much as a thousand years older than the Psalms. Their religious epics, such as the story of Istar's descent into Hades, and the epic of Gilgamesh, in which various experi-ences in the land of shades or in the lower world are re-lated, bear witness to their belief in a future life.

Some of the oldest literature in the world is found in the Egyptian "Book of the Dead." Belief in immortality is a prominent feature in that literature. The Egyptians be-lieved that the soul could not enjoy immortality unless the body itself were preserved. The huge pyramids and rock-hewn tombs in the land of the Nile and the careful embalm-ing of the dead show to what great lengths they went to preserve the body for the return of the spirit. The corpse (or mummy) was provided with a copy of the Book of the Dead and the papyrus-roll containing the prayer he was to offer and the chart of his journey through the unseen world. The departed was even spoken of as "the living," and the coffin as "the chest of the living." The life beyond, particularly the punishments of the wicked, was described in vivid terms.

Only recently in Egypt (June, 1954) there was discovered the burial chamber of the Pharaoh Cheops which was sealed about 5,000 years ago, in which was found the solar boat that he had built for his journey through the heavens at night, together with the magic hieroglyphic incantations and hymns prescribed to pass him safely along on his eternal voyage with the great sun god Ra. In Egypt practically all travel from one part of the country to another was on the Nile, and from prehistoric times the Egyptians thought of boats as the natural and only means of travel, both in life and after death.

The following interesting explanation of the solar boats has been given by El-Malakh, director of archeological work for the Egyptian government:

"The great tomb builders took fantastic pains to preserve the solar boats which they believed necessary to join the caravan of immortals gathered around Ra and journeying with him through his daily death and rebirth .... The day boats were used for travel with Ra from the dawn, where he was reborn, to the western gates of the underworld, where he died at each sunset. The immortals all changed there to their solar boats of the night for the terrifying nocturnal trip through the underworld. The boats had to pass twelve gates, representing hours, on each leg of the journey, twenty-four in all, by saying a secret name of the guardian god. These secret names were imparted after death to good souls. Proper hymns and incantations had to be recited to insure safety."

In India the records of Hinduism and Brahmanism, as set forth in the Rig-Veda, reveal a clear belief in immortality. More than a thousand hymns are found in that collection, some of them going back to a period ten to fifteen centuries before Christ. Buddhism, which was a later development from Hinduism, introduced the idea of transmigration of souls, in which it was held that the person who died was immediately re-born, his new state being determined by the degree of reward or punishment due him. The highest goal was union with Brahma, which might mean extinction but in other cases continued re-births. The one to whom punishment was due might be re-born as a slave, or an animal, or bird, or even as a reptile or insect. This was called transmigration of souls, and was widely held in both India and Persia. A weariness of existence was one of the features of this belief, the only escape from which was conceived to be absolute extinction, — in which belief it stands at the opposite extreme from Christianity. Whereas Christianity offers the blessedness of eternal life in heaven, Buddhism offers what it calls the blessedness of extinction.

In Persia Zoroastrianism set forth a dualism throughout all nature. Ormuzd, the spirit of goodness and light, and Ahriman, the spirit of evil and darkness, were struggling for the mastery. Every man inevitably had to take part in that struggle. If he chose good he was rewarded with eternal life. Much absurdity was mingled with the ideas of immortality, judgment, paradise, hell, and a restored earth, although the system assumes the eventual victory of good over evil.

In the ancient Greek religion there was a belief in many gods and in a future life. The early views of Hades were very gloomy, and the future life in general was conceived of pretty much as an attenuated edition of earthly existence. A silver coin was placed in the mouth of the corpse to pay his fare across the mystic river. Their philosophers felt the natural longing in the human heart for some kind of existence beyond the narrow span of life. They spoke vaguely of an underworld and of a probable immortality, but they had no grounds of assurance.

In Rome the worshippers of Jupiter and Minerva looked forward to the shadowy realm of the dead, the misty region of the grave, about which they knew little, but in which they firmly believed. In China and Japan belief in immortality took the form of ancestor worship.

The American Indians placed within the grave of the departed one his bow and arrows, and sometimes his pony, that he might have these when he reached the happy hunting ground. The Norsemen provided the dead hero with a horse and armor for his triumphant ride, and in Greenland the deceased Eskimo child was provided with a dog to act as its guide.

Some of the orientals taught, and still teach, a form of pantheism, in which the human soul is absorbed into one universal personality. Materialistic philosophy, in both ancient and modern times, which of course can scarcely be called a religion, has held that there is no surviving personality after death. It holds that at death the soul of man is like the flame of a candle that is snuffed out, that man dies as the animals and the plants, and that nothing remains but dust and ashes. There are not many professed materialists in our day, but there are millions of *practical* materialists, who have no reasoned convictions on the subject and who live as though death ended all. Their attitude toward life is well summed up in the motto, "Let us eat, drink and be merry, for tomorrow we die."

3. Immortality Necessary to Vindicate the Moral Order

There must be a future life in order that the justice of God may be vindicated. In this life so much good goes unrewarded, and so much evil goes unpunished. If there were no other reasons the demands of the justice of God would be sufficient to prove the case. Otherwise the moral order of the universe would not be right.

So often we see the wicked succeed, get unjust gain, have so many of this world's good things, and apparently have a far better time of it than their neighbors or associates who try to keep the commandments of God and to whom life is not always kind. Often we see truth dragged in the dust and wrong seated on the throne. We see a Nero in the palace and a Paul in the dungeon. Think of the injustices so often done in our courts to those falsely accused. Think of those who escape just punishment for their crimes. Think of the injustices in business between employers and employees, between sellers and purchasers. In many homes those who are weak are the victims of cruelty and oppression. The righteous so often suffer reverses, lose their health and their possessions, are oppressed and persecuted. So often these things seem to happen to the wrong people. Viewed from the standpoint of this world, these things represent gross injustice. It is unreasonable to think that those who in this life escape just punishment shall escape forever, or that the good services of the righteous shall be forever unrewarded. Rather it is the unalterable law that "Whatsoever a man soweth, that shall he also reap"; and if he does not reap it in this life he must do so in the life to come.

To deny the future life is to open wide the gate for all kinds of indulgence and crime. If death ends everything life in this world becomes a mockery, and the person who can secure for himself the most pleasure regardless of the means used is the most successful, the most to be envied. As Paul expresses it, "If we have only hoped in Christ in this life, we are of all men most pitiable," I Cor. 15:19.

Our reason rebels against the thought that a system in which sin and injustice and suffering are so prominent can have death as the end of all things. The answer to the sins and injustices and unrewarded services of this life is a future life in which there must be a "judgment to come," such as that which terrified Felix when Paul preached to him (Acts 24:25), a future life in which righteousness and

holiness will be the order of all things. Mere extinction of
being would not be a sufficient penalty for the evil, nor a fit
reward for the righteous. Bluntly expressed, If there is a
just God, there must be a future life. "Shall not the Judge
of all the earth do right?" Gen. 18:25. No just God could
allow a system in which so much evil goes unpunished and
so much good unrewarded.

4. Life Here Is Incomplete

Another strong evidence for immortality is the fact that
this present life even at its best is so incomplete. The
greater part of man's work always seems to remain unfinished. So many of his talents and skills are never developed
at all, and the ones he does acquire are hardly developed
to a high degree of efficiency until he is taken away. We
instinctively feel that there *ought* to be a future life in
which these can be brought to perfection and adequate use
made of them. The minister, teacher, statesman, lawyer
or scientist spends a lifetime accumulating the knowledge
and experience that should enable him to proceed as a master in his field, but soon his life is cut short. Similarly the
surgeon, musician and artist reach the heights only after
a lifetime of study and practice. If there be no hereafter
that valuable knowledge and skill is lost forever. Life here
is too short, too circumscribed, to be the end for man's
marvelous divinely given endowments and aspirations. He
scarcely more than gets his preparations made for full and
intelligent living until his time comes to leave. The truly
great scientist feels that he has not mastered the one-
hundredth part of the knowledge that is to be known in his
field. As he surveys a library of books on his particular
field, what a small fraction of that knowledge he feels that
he really possesses! Thomas Edison late in life expressed
himself as feeling as if he were but a small boy playing
along the beach, picking up and examining a pebble here,
and another there, while the limitless expanse of coast-
line and ocean stretched out before him. The farther one

goes in his chosen profession the smaller his knowledge seems in comparison with the vast fields that open up before him. What scientist or scholar worthy of the name has not felt the inadequacy and limitations, of his present endeavor? Without immortality the whole process of knowledge and accomplishment is thwarted.

A good and intelligent man does not immediately destroy the masterpiece that he has made. Suppose that a great artist after finishing a beautiful picture should take his knife and cut it to shreds. Or that a great sculptor after finishing a beautiful statue should take his hammer and break it to pieces. Would not mankind indict him for a lack of intelligence, or for irrationality? Surely a good and wise Creator will not finish His masterpiece, which is man, and then so soon destroy him. To attribute such action to God is to attribute to Him a lower order of intelligence than we find in His creatures. If God is good and wise, as He certainly is, and if life has the meaning that we are compelled to believe that it has, then it is incredible that life should have been summoned out of the void only to be so soon returned to the void from whence it came.

If human life consisted only of the time that lies between birth and death it would be but a truncated and largely futile thing. The broken column, resting on a base but reaching nowhere, is a fitting symbol to express the incompleteness of life in this world.

The present life, even at its best, does not satisfy. There are, of course, many pleasures, but often these are only temporary and deceptive. The truth is that from the richest mansion to the poorest hut each person has his own peculiar combination of worries, fears, sorrows, toils, sicknesses and disappointments. Man, who was created in the image of God and who therefore has limitless possibilities, surely was destined for something better than this. Apart from the satisfaction that a person receives from the knowledge that he has rendered a true service or accomplished something worth while, probably no one at the end of his

life course would want to live his life over a second time
if it meant going through exactly the same experiences.
Who would want to live even yesterday over again?

Man's soaring ambitions and his longing for a greater
freedom are indications that he was created for a higher
life. When, for instance, we see a great eagle confined in a
cage, his wings trailing the ground as he walks, we know
that that lordly creature was never meant to spend his life
in that cage. The Creator who gave him those mighty pin-
ions intended that they should serve to carry him away
into the boundless spaces of the far distances. The same
Creator who designed that eagle's whole nature for the
wide open sky likewise made us for a larger sphere than
we are able to find here.

As the organization of the fish implies water as the element in which it shall live and move, and as that of the
bird implies air, so the existence of spiritual and moral and
intellectual powers within man implies a fit environment
in which he shall be free to develop and perfect those powers. Surely God did not bring the human spirit to such a
high degree of development as is attained by man, for no
other purpose than to allow it to lapse again into nothing-
ness. We are creatures of time, but we are destined for
eternity. We long for that greater holiness, that fuller
vision, that more perfect hearing, and that more rapid
means of communication and transportation. How inscru-
table and meaningless must be human life and destiny to
the natural man who has no revelation to guide him
through the labyrinth of this world!!

Man's life in this world is but the preliminary stage, the
training school as it were, to prepare him for the really
serious business of living. Always there are so many glar-
ing deficiencies and failures, and so many other things that
we feel should be added to make life full and complete.
Looking back over our mistakes and blunders and lost opportunities we feel that this time we have hardly more than
learned *how* to live, and that, humanly speaking, if we

could live our lives over again we could accomplish so much more. As for doing that which God has commanded us to do, all of us have been "unprofitable servants," at best having done only that which it was our duty to do (Luke 17:10). We are like new recruits in the army, or more particularly like new cadets in the air force, — more of a handicap than a help until our training is complete and we find our places in the larger organization.

The grave, then, is not a blind alley, but a thoroughfare, leading to a much richer life beyond. This life is but prologue; the primary sphere of our existence lies in the future. We can attain completeness only in that other realm where there is no more sickness nor death and where progress is always onward and upward.

It should be kept in mind, of course, that in saying these things we are thinking of life as it should be lived, with its high spiritual import. For the wicked, immortality means eternal death, that is, eternal separation from God. Whereas the course of the righteous is always onward and upward to greater blessedness and accomplishment, the course of the wicked is always downward into greater and more awful sin. What a solemn thought it is, that every child born into this world is a spiritual being who will go on living for ever either in heaven or in hell!

5. The Argument from Analogy

It is to be acknowledged, of course, that in formal logic the argument from analogy does not afford positive proof. The fact that two things are similar in one respect is not in itself proof that they are similar in another. Nevertheless, a true analogy does give a high degree of probability, and it is a valid argument within its proper sphere.

There are many analogies in nature which point clearly to a resurrection and new life. In the autumn, for instance, nature seems to die. The flowers fade. The leaves fall from the trees and the grass withers. Most of the bird and insect life departs, and soon the earth is covered with a cold blanket of snow and ice. Life seems to be over; death seems to have conquered, to be the master. But in due time the spring comes, and with it warm air and new life. The barren trees put forth new buds and leaves. The buried seeds, which looked so dry and lifeless, germinate, send up new plants, and put forth gorgeous fragrant flowers. The grass becomes green, and the birds return and are heard on every hand. The caterpillar or larva comes out of its rough and unsightly cocoon and develops into the beautiful butterfly or highly colored moth. Throughout nature the dormant stage gives way to the growing stage. That which appeared to be dead is alive again; all nature seems to rejoice.

And what is the purpose of this annual pageant? For one thing, does not God speak to man through nature, telling him of a better and more enduring life after death? Does not Paul tell us that "the invisible things of him since the creation of the world are clearly seen, being perceived through the things that are made?" Rom. 1:20. The psalmist says: "The heavens declare the glory of God; And the firmament showeth his handiwork. Day unto day uttereth speech, And night unto night showeth knowledge," Ps. 19:1, 2. We can indeed learn much from the general revelation that is given through nature to supplement the special revelation that is given through Scripture.

It is an axiom of science that no material object in the universe can be destroyed. That which disappears in one form reappears in another, either in the form of matter or of energy. The log is burned, and disappears as a log. But the scientist can prove that every particle of that log continues to exist although in a different form. When the person dies the body, too, returns to its elements, but is not destroyed. This law operates everywhere throughout nature. If, then, the material of man's body continues to exist, surely the life, which is of infinitely greater value, must be going on somewhere. Surely God in His wisdom and goodness would not preserve the lower elements of His creation and permit the higher to perish.

6. Immortality an Innate Idea

The natural longing of mankind for continued existence is inexplicable if it is not founded on reality. A belief that is age-long and world-wide is not to be set aside lightly. In this connection we must keep in mind that not all of our knowledge is received through the physical senses. There are some basic truths, — innate or intuitive truths, we call them, — that are given to man by creation, ideas that arise from the constitution of the mind, as contrasted with others that are acquired through experience. These truths may be further developed in life by the knowledge that comes through experience, but they are not in themselves dependent on experience. One such truth is belief in God. Another is the moral sense of right and wrong. Still another is that with which we are presently concerned, belief in a future life or in the immortality of the soul. There never has been a tribe discovered anywhere, even among the most primitive people, that did not have these three basic beliefs.

Along with these three ideas there commonly are associated four more that are necessary in man's reasoning processes. These are: the idea of time, of space, of number, and of cause and effect. Not one of these needs to be taught, nor is any one of them originally derived from experience. Where they are ignored or denied only confusion can result.

These innate ideas correspond to that which in the animal and bird and insect kingdom is known as "instinct." No one ever needs to teach nor can teach the beaver how to construct a dam across a stream, nor the birds how to build their nests or to migrate with the seasons, nor the honey bee how to construct the comb in order to store the honey most efficiently. In the human species the presence of innate ideas does not mean that children are born with these beliefs, but rather that as they develop toward years of

accountability these basic truths are instinctively recognized and are capable of being developed into more consistent systems.

Why, then, some one may ask, does it happen that some
few develop into atheists, or appear to have no clear idea
of right or wrong, or disbelieve in the immortality of the
soul? The first and primary reason is that man is no longer in the highly favored state in which he was created, in
which his nature functioned normally, but is now a victim of sin and of unsound reason. In his fallen state he is at
enmity with God. He no longer has a clear and unprejudiced mind with which to judge moral and spiritual values. He does not want to acknowledge a Creator, or a
moral Lawgiver, or to face the prospect of existence in a
future state in which he receives punishment for his sins.
He would gladly be rid of all these beliefs, and he attempts
to argue himself into believing that these things do not
exist. Not until he is regenerated by the Holy Spirit and
given a new principle of spiritual life is he able to judge
clearly concerning moral and spiritual values.

That this is the condition of fallen man as set forth in
Scripture is beyond question. In the first chapter of Romans Paul points out the depth of moral and spiritual de-
generation into which man has fallen, vss. 18-32. In I Cor.
2:14 he shows why it is impossible for fallen man to arrive at spiritual truth by his own efforts: "Now the natural
man receiveth not the things of the Spirit of God; for they
are foolishness unto him; and he cannot know them, because they are spiritually judged." This was also brought
out when he said: "But we preach Christ crucified, unto
Jews a stumbling block, and unto Gentiles foolishness; but
unto them that are called, both Jews and Greeks, Christ
the power of God and the wisdom of God," I Cor. 1:23,24.
And Christ Himself said, "Except one be born anew he
cannot see the kingdom of God," John 3:3.

A second and less important reason for the denial of
these intuitive truths is that when they are approached

from the viewpoint of the physical sciences the tendency oftentimes is to accept as truth only that which can be scientifically demonstrated or that which is based on experience. More will be said about this in the following chapter.

7. Proof Not to Be Obtained from Science or Philosophy

In the study of immortality our primary source of information cannot be either Science or Philosophy. Science can view these things only from the limited viewpoint of the material world, and can accept only that testimony which comes through the physical senses. It is therefore unable to deal with the basic issue, and can give no real assurance either for or against immortality. Among individual scientists many professing the Christian faith have asserted their belief in immortality, while others not holding the Christian faith have often been inclined to doubt or even to deny that the soul continues after death.

No person can "prove" or "demonstrate" immortality by scientific experiment or mathematical formula any more than he can prove or demonstrate the existence of God by such means. Men act thoughtlessly when they demand such proof. The so-called rational proofs may furnish a strong presumption in favor of the existence of God, or of immortality, and they usually will be accepted as proof by the spiritually enlightened. But they do not amount to absolute demonstration and therefore are not strong enough to compel belief on the part of the unregenerate soul.

The reason for this is that the facts of the spiritual world cannot be perceived by the physical senses, but are "spiritually discerned." When the physical senses attempt to handle the things of the spirit, they step beyond their legitimate boundaries and invade a realm concerning which they can speak with no authority. The intellect, too, is a part of "the natural man," having acquired a bias against moral and spiritual things as a result of the fall, and is no more capable of interpreting the realities of the spiritual realm than are the physical senses. Evidence for immortality must be, in the very nature of the case, inward and subjective. The worldly, unregenerate man cannot see it; the godly, spiritual man cannot fail to see it. The one who lives a life worthy of immortality will find little difficulty in believing in immortality, and his conviction of it will grow as he grows in grace.

Physical science as such cannot tell us anything about immortality, for it deals only with tangible things, that is, with life and phenomena in the physical world. The only answer that it can give to the question of immortality is a profound silence. Concerning the unseen spiritual world it knows nothing and has no way of finding out. Materialistic science often refuses even to admit that the soul is a life principle independent of the body until positive sensory evidence is given. But that is asking too much. Since the body and the soul belong to different spheres, it is unreasonable to seek sensory evidence in the body as confirmation of the reality of the soul. That position is as unreasonable as for a blind man to deny that there is any such thing as light, for the simple reason that he cannot see it. The difficulty is not with the light but in the fact that he does not have the right organ. True and unprejudiced science declares only that it can give neither proof nor disproof of the spiritual, and that so far as it is concerned the spiritual must be dealt with as an unverified hypothesis.

Nor can philosophy give much if any more aid than science. It too must work within the limitations of the human mind, and, also like science, it has no source of information outside of the world itself. Whereas theology is God's explanation of the world, its origin, purpose and destiny, given through an inspired book, the Bible, philosophy is man's explanation, confined within the limitations of the human mind and the material world. No philosopher has ever been able to solve the riddle of the universe, nor has any been able to find a remedy for sin.

In the past the denial of immortality has arisen primarily from a materialistic philosophy. This has been true even though most of those denying immortality have had no formal connection with or understanding of philosophy as such. It is quite evident that if we rule out the existence of God and start with the premise that originally matter alone existed, the dualistic conception of man as a soul united with a body must be given up. For in that case mental activity becomes merely a function of the brain, and ceases when the brain is destroyed. Hence the importance of the question, *What is man?* Is he a being originally created in the image of God, possessed of body and spirit and destined for an immortal future? Or is he the product of organic evolution, coming into existence in the most elementary form in which life can exist and gradually developing into the self-conscious, reasoning being of his present stage?

The answer that we give to these questions will determine largely the views we hold regarding the immortality of the soul. The standard illustration employed by materialistic philosophy to illustrate the phenomena of thought processes in man is that of the electric generator producing current: — as the generator produces current, so the brain produces thought; when the generator stops the current ceases, and when the body dies the soul ceases to exist. If we accept the premise of materialistic philosophy and rule out God as the First Cause and Creator, we must also accept its conclusion that man is a product of material forces, and that he has reached his present high position through a process of organic evolution.

Precisely what do we mean by organic evolution? Probably the most scientific definition is that given by the geologist Le Conte. Said he: "Evolution is (1) a continuous progressive change, (2) according to certain laws, and (3) by means of resident forces."

It should hardly need to be said that the theory of evolution. which is so widely held today, is a philosophical. not

a scientific theory. Science deals with *facts*, with that
which we *know*, as the derivation of the word indicates, —
that which can be demonstrated in the laboratory. Philosophy includes the much broader field of theory and hypothesis. There is no scientific proof whatever that life ever
has been produced from non-living matter, nor that one
species has ever changed into another, nor is there any
proof of the extremely primitive condition through which
it is alleged that man rose to his present position. "To
talk of the evolution of thought from sea-slime to amoeba,
and from amoeba to a self-conscious man," says Louis T.
More, "means nothing; it is the easy solution of the thought-
less mind . . . . Let the biologist in the laboratory produce
a living cell which has not been derived from other living
matter. Until he creates a living cell from dead matter he
is in the same class as was Aristotle who tells us that dust
breeds fleas."[13]

For an analysis displaying unusual insight into the
problems before us we quote from the writings of Dr. C.
B. McMullen, Professor Emeritus of Centre College, himself a philosopher and the author of a particularly cogent
book on this subject, *The Logic of Evolution*. In a recently
prepared but as yet unpublished manuscript he says:

"Where shall we find an adequate solution of the problems that are our greatest concern? Certainly not in the
conflicting philosophies that have been worked out down
through the ages. They are usually departmental philosophies that have been extended beyond their own boundaries.

"That is true of the philosophy of naturalism, which is
held by most scientists. In ethics, it has reduced the moral
law to 'behaviour patterns,' which are based on expediency.
In Theology, it has resulted in Modernism which has elim-
inated the supernatural from the Scriptures in varying degrees, from little to all.

13. *The Dogma of Evolution*, pp. 244, 247.

"Reduced to a formula, the view commonly held by materialistic scientists — and developed as a whole or in part by modernistic theologians — runs somewhat as follows: Our world begun as nebulous matter; that, in time, manifested itself in chemical activity, and this, in time, rose to the level of life in plants, came to consciousness in animals, and emerged into self-consciousness in man. In short, that which was originally nothing but matter, ruled by physical force, at length attained to intelligence enough to produce sky-scrapers and atom bombs.

"It is well to remember that in a materialistic philosophy there is no place for the supernatural, either in the past or in the future. Man is entirely on his own. He is simply an accident — merely an accident — in the cosmic process. Materialism knows no freedom; and without freedom there can be no responsibility. Right and wrong have no moral meaning in a materialistic universe. Expediency has replaced them. Conscience is but a trick of nature adopted to make social life possible and to save us from mutual slaughter."[14]

The moral and spiritual decline that inevitably follows in the wake of an evolutionary philosophy is summed up in the well chosen words of William H. Wood: "The case that is made out against evolution and its devotees especially within the Church is a serious one. Evolution dispenses not only with faith but with the God of faith. The hypothesis 'God' seems not to be needed. Revelation is denied, the authority of Scripture is impugned, miracles are laughed out of court, man is deposed from the high estate given him by the Bible and rated merely as a noble animal, naturalism is the accepted philosophy, freedom is made a clever deception, and immortality applies only to the stuff of the human body."[15]

A case very much to the point is the recently discovered hoax of the Piltdown skull, for the past forty years accep-

14. *Aids To Bible Study.*
15. *The Religion of Science*, p. 3.

ted by evolutionary scientists as a 100,000 year old relic of prehistoric man. Those bones were found in a gravel pit near the southern coast of England, and have been on exhibit in the British natural history museum, in London, as one of the primary proofs of the theory of evolution. But the museum has now published a booklet (January, 1955) by twelve experts which states that the jaw bone and some of the teeth are those of an immature ape, that they have been doctored to resemble human bones, and that even the flint instruments alleged to have been found with the bones also were frauds.

8. Scripture Teaching Regarding Immortality

The only reliable information concerning the state of the soul after death is to be found in the Bible. That which the philosophers cannot fathom, nor the scientists explain, God has revealed in His Word. Much is presented by direct statement; much also is assumed as undeniably true and not needing proof. In general the Bible treats the subject of the immortality of the soul in much the same way that it treats the existence of God, — such belief is assumed as an undeniable postulate. It takes for granted that the characteristics of our nature are permanent, that we shall continue to possess intelligence, affection, conscience and will. Every passage dealing with the future life assumes that we shall be then as we are now, reverential and social beings, loving God and one another. This necessarily includes recognition, communion with Christ and with the angels and the redeemed.

What, then, does the Bible teach concerning the immortality of the soul? We look first at: —

The Old Testament. In Gen. 5:24 we read: "And Enoch walked with God: and he was not, for God took him"; — and in Heb. 11:5 we read, "By faith Enoch was translated that he should not see death." One of the most familiar Old Testament expressions is that of being "gathered to their people," — Abraham, Gen. 15:15; 25:8; Isaac, Gen. 35:29; Jacob, Gen. 49:33; etc.

Job asked the question, "If a man die, shall he live again?" 14:14, and himself emphatically answered that question in the affirmative: "But as for me I know that my Redeemer liveth, And at last he will stand up upon the earth: And after my skin, even this body, is destroyed Then without my flesh shall I see God," 19:25,26.

David, "the sweet singer of Israel," believed in immortality, for he said: "Thou wilt not leave my soul to Sheol; Neither wilt thou suffer thy holy one to see corruption," Ps. 16:10; — and in the New Testament Peter applies these words to the resurrection of Christ: ". . . he foreseeing this spake of the resurrection of Christ," Acts 2:31. David also said, "In thy presence is fulness of joy; In thy right hand there are pleasures for evermore," Ps. 16:11; and, "I shall behold thy face in righteousness; I shall be satisfied, when I awake, with beholding thy form," Ps. 17:15. The 23rd Psalm teaches immortality and describes it as walking through the valley of the shadow of death without fear, and closes with the assurance, "And I shall dwell in the house of the Lord forever." In Ps. 73:1-19 the psalmist (Asaph) points to life beyond the grave to explain why in this life virtue should so often fail to be rewarded while the wicked so often prosper, declaring that he was envious at the arrogant when he saw the prosperity of the wicked, until he went into the sanctuary of God and saw their latter end. Verses 24 and 25 of this same psalm read, "Thou wilt guide me with thy counsel, And afterward receive me into glory. Whom have I in heaven but thee? And there is none upon earth that I desire besides thee."

David's hope of seeing his child who had died was expressed in these words: "I shall go to him, but he will not return to me," II Sam. 12:23. Solomon believed in immortality, for he wrote: "He hath set eternity in their heart," Eccl. 3:11; and again, "The dust returneth to the earth as it was, and the spirit returneth to God who gave it," Eccl. 12:7.

Immortality was taught very explicitly in the prophets. In Isaiah we read: "Thy dead shall live; my dead bodies shall arise. Awake and sing, ye that dwell in the dust: for thy dew is as the dew of herbs, and the earth shall cast forth the dead," 26:19. Daniel said: "And many of them that sleep in the dust of the earth shall awake, some to everlasting life, and some to shame and everlasting contempt. And they that be wise shall shine as the brightness of the firmament; and they that turn many to righteousness as the stars for ever and ever," Dan. 12:2,3. And God speaking through Hosea said: "I will ransom them from the power of Sheol; I will redeem them from death," 13:14.

The New Testament. While the doctrine of immortality is set forth clearly in the Old Testament, its unveiling is complete in the New Testament. In fact it there seems to be on almost every page. Jesus came to a people who believed in a future life. One group only, the Sadducees, who were the materialistic skeptics of that day, disbelieved it (Matt. 22:23). Christ's work of redemption was performed for that purpose. His whole outlook on life was based on it. He lived in the very atmosphere of eternity, and life in the other world was as real to Him as was life in this world. So much fuller and more advanced was His teaching over that of the old dispensation that Paul could say that it was "our Saviour Jesus Christ, who abolished death, and brought life and immortality to light through the gospel," II Tim. 1:10.

Job's question, "If a man die, shall he live again?" finds its answer in the words of Christ: "I am the resurrection, and the life: he that believeth on me, though he die, yet shall he live; and whosoever liveth and believeth on me shall never die," John 11:25,26.

Other representative New Testament statements are: "God gave unto us eternal life, and this life is in the Son. He that hath the Son hath the life; he that hath not the Son of God hath not the life," I John 5:11, 12. "And be not afraid of them that kill the body, but are not able to kill the soul; but rather fear him who is able to destroy both soul and body in hell," Matt. 10:28. "The hour cometh, in which all that are in the tombs shall hear his voice, and shall come forth; they that have done good, unto the resurrection of life; and they that have done evil, unto the resurrection of judgment," John 5:28,29. "For God so loved the world, that he gave his only begotten Son, that whosoever believeth on him should not perish, but have eternal life," John 3:16. "I go to prepare a place for you . . . that where I am, there ye may be also," John 14:2,3.

The most impressive and conclusive of all proofs of immortality is the resurrection of Christ. This affords the supreme proof of life beyond the grave. "I was dead, and behold, I am alive for evermore, and I have the keys of death and of Hades," Rev. 1:18. He declared the truth and then by His resurrection demonstrated the fact of life beyond the grave. Before the year 1492 many people had speculated about a trans-Atlantic continent. But those speculations in themselves were of little value. Quite different, however, were the proofs that Columbus brought back showing that he had actually visited a new world beyond the seas. Similarly, Christ by His resurrection has given the most convincing proof that life does go on after death. From the beginning of time many thoughtful souls had been saying that there must be another life. Even among the pagans that hope had been expressed in various forms of religion and practice. The best of the philosophers, Socrates and Plato, had died with the hope of immortality on their lips. The Old Testament prophets had declared the fact quite clearly. But when Christ died and then actually came back from the land beyond the grave, the world had the proof that its hopes were based on reality.

Paul's teaching is, of course, in full harmony with that of Christ. "For I reckon that the sufferings of this present

time are not worthy to be compared with the glory which
shall be revealed to us-ward," Rom. 8:18. "For our light
affliction, which is for the moment, worketh for us more
and more exceedingly an eternal weight of glory; while
we look not at the things which are seen, but at the things
which are not seen: for the things which are seen are tem-
poral; but the things which are not seen are eternal," II
Cor. 4:17,18. "I have fought the good fight, I have finished
the course, I have kept the faith: henceforth there is laid
up for me the crown of righteousness, which the Lord, the
righteous judge, shall give to me in that day; and not to me
only, but also to all them that have loved his appearing," II
Tim. 4:7,8. In II Cor. 5:1 Paul compares the body to a habitation, from which we depart at death: "We know that if
the earthly house of our tabernacle be dissolved, we have
a building from God, a house not made with hands, eternal,
in the heavens."

The writer of the Epistle to the Hebrews says that Abraham had this faith, for when God commanded him to offer up his only son, Isaac, in whom all of his hopes were
centered, he obeyed, "accounting that God is able to raise
up, even from the dead; from whence he did also in a figure
receive him back," Heb. 11:19. The Bible is unmistakably
clear in teaching that man does have an immortal soul and
that he shall live for ever and ever.

9. Wholesome Results that Flow from a Belief in Immortality

What a source of joy and satisfaction the anticipation
of the future life is even here in this world! The saint who
is well-nigh exhausted under the burden of earthly care and
responsibility can and does look away with pleasure to that
happy home. What a sense of comfort the hope of immortality brings to the sick, the persecuted, the neglected and
the aged! They may actually shout for joy as they foresee
the glad hour when they shall enter into rest, when "sorrow
and sighing shall flee away."

The anticipation of the future life should not be such that it interferes with our faithfulness to our present work, nor should it make us discontented to continue our life here. The balance between these two motives that was attained by the Apostle Paul would seem to be the ideal. On one occasion he had been caught up to the third heaven and his soul filled with the most rapturous experience of bliss. That experience remained with him during the remainder of his earthly life, and it gave him an assurance that could not be shaken by any amount of hardship or persecution. He longed for the heavenly life, yet he was conscious of an urgent duty to be performed toward his fellow men, — "But I am in a strait betwixt the two, having the desire to depart and be with Christ; for it is very far better; yet to abide in the flesh is more needful for your sake," Phil. 1:23,24.

Under normal conditions all of us love life and seek to preserve it as long as possible. Whether in plenty or in want, in health or in sickness, in joy or in sorrow, we value life as our most precious possession and cling to it until the very end. It is only proper, therefore, that as long as God gives us life we should accept it joyfully and proceed to the tasks before us, in order that we may accomplish as much as possible while the day of opportunity lasts.

The doctrine of immortality makes us aware that we are but temporary residents in this world. It was never intended that we should settle down here as permanent citizens. Paul says, "Our citizenship is in heaven," Phil. 3:20. After we are converted we are detained here in the capacity of witnesses to others, and in order that as we witness we may grow in grace and sanctification in preparation for the life beyond. When our assigned task is finished we should be ready to answer the call to the higher realm. Our reward in heaven will be in proportion to the faithfulness of our service here.

Where this doctrine has been taught its tendency has been to develop and uplift mankind. Men who pass under its sway receive visions not only of the greatness of a future life, but the present life is caused to take on a new meaning. In providing as a goal a future life in which virtue, honesty and holiness receive their appropriate rewards it is a strong aid to, if indeed not an essential of, real human progress. We may also point out that the reason there is so much unbridled sin and crime is because those who engage in such things do not believe in a resurrection and a future judgment, or that for the time being at least they succeed in keeping those thoughts out of mind. Some one has well said, "There is nothing more conducive to immorality than a disbelief in immortality." Let people believe that there is no life beyond the grave, no meeting of a righteous God in judgment, and they throw off the normal restraints. Their tendency then is to give themselves over to the passions of the flesh and the mind, and to trample upon the rights of their fellow men. Fear of punishment is not the highest motive to morality, but it is an effective one, and where it is absent crime soon becomes rampant.

Nor is it sufficient to believe in some attenuated or spurious form of immortality, such as the continued existence of the race as one generation follows another, or the moral judgment for good or evil that posterity passes on the individual. To say that the race is immortal but that the individual is not, is to deny the only kind of immortality that can have any real meaning. True, the trees and flowers cover the earth from generation to generation. But the answer to that is that the same tree lives but once, and the same flower blooms but once. The individual person lives in this world but once, and if that were the end there would be no real immortality for him. Furthermore, the race as such has no consciousness. Consciousness is the property of the individual only.

As for the moral judgment passed on the individual by posterity, surely the righteous deserve more than a good name, and the wicked more than a bad name. Nor is the thought expressed in the lines of George Eliot any better:

"O may I join the choir invisible
Of those immortal dead who live again
In minds made better by their presence."

It is, of course, nice to live on in the minds and hearts of a grateful posterity. But, as just said, that is not immortality at all in the true sense of the term. If that were all, most of us would not live very long. It is only rarely that the deceased is remembered by any great number. Those who so stand out in the history of any nation are few indeed. It is to be noticed further that immortality of influence applies to the evil as well as to the good.

There is no adequate basis for the assertion made by some that immortality on the part of man implies also immortality on the part of animals, — that the dog, being a living creature, is therefore as immortal as his master. The difference between men and animals is such that the immortality of the former would seem to exclude that of the latter. Man is a self-conscious, moral being. He knows the difference between right and wrong. He has a sense of the existence of God, and of the reality of sin when he offends against God. His being therefore demands a future life in which he shall receive rewards or punishments. But the animal has none of these attributes. It has no real moral nature. Its actions are governed primarily by instinct and habit. It has consciousness, but not self-consciousness. It cannot say to itself, "Here am I." It therefore is not a thinking being. The basic features of man's nature are radically different from those of the animal.

This, however, does not necessarily mean that in heaven there will be no animal or bird or plant life. What would the present earth be like without these? No doubt part of the glory of the renewed earth will be a restored and rejuvenated animal and plant life that will reflect the beauty of that realm. Paul's statement that "the whole creation groaneth and travaileth in pain together until now," and the immediately following words, "And not only so, but ourselves also . . . groan within ourselves, waiting for our adoption, to wit, the redemption of our body," (Rom. 8:22, 23), would seem to indicate that the lower orders of creation suffer as a result of the fall of man and that they are to share in the glory that is to be revealed. While we cannot speak with certainty in this regard, we apparently are safe in concluding that as in this present world one generation of plants and animals succeeds another, so in the new earth there will be plant and animal life, no doubt much more luxurious and varied and permanent than here, but that the individual ones that we have known will not be there.

The practical lesson that all of this teaches is a very solemn one: the obligation that rests on each person to make his life worthy of immortality. For obviously what is needed to make immortality a desirable thing is not mere continuance of life, but a better quality of life. If another life is to follow this one, then the seventy or eighty years spent on this earth is as but a fleeting moment when compared with eternity. The endlessness of eternity is more than our minds can grasp. Even the life of a Methuselah, who lived 969 years, is insignificantly short. It becomes obvious that there is something vastly more important than making one's self powerful, or comfortable, or secure on earth. Life should resolve itself into the problem of developing the only thing that one can take with him when he leaves this earth, — character.

The noted British scientist, Professor Huxley, like many another who became absorbed with material things, could see little hope of the future. On his tomb were inscribed the following words:

"And if there be no meeting past the grave,
If all is darkness, silence, yet 't is rest.
For God still giveth his beloved sleep,
And if an endless sleep he wills, so best."

Darkness — silence — endless sleep; not much consolation there, except for those who would escape a guilty conscience. Contrast with this the comfort found in the words of Christ: "Let not your heart be troubled; believe in God, believe also in me. In my Father's house are many mansions; if it were not so, I would have told you; for I go to prepare a place for you. And if I go and prepare a place for you, I will come again, and will receive you unto myself; that where I am, there ye may be also," John 14:1-3.

The Homegoing of Valiant-for-Truth as a good soldier in Bunyan's *Pilgrim's Progress* is applicable here. It reads:

"After this it was noised abroad that Mr. Valiant-for-Truth was taken with a summons by the same post as the other. When he understood it, he called his friends and told them of it. Then, said he, 'I am going to my Father's; and though with great difficulty I am got hither, yet now I do not repent me of all the trouble I have been at to arrive where I am. My sword I give to him that shall succeed me in my pilgrimage, and my courage and skill to him that can get it. My marks and scars I carry with me, to be a witness for me, that I have fought His battles who now will be my rewarder.'

"When the day that he must go hence was come, many accompanied him to the river side into which as he went he said, 'Death, where is thy sting?' And as he went down deeper, he said, 'Grave, where is thy victory?' So he passed over, and all the trumpets sounded for him on the other side."

At the grave, not Tolstoi's forlorn "Goodbye for ever," but the beautiful German *Auf wiedersehn*—"We shall meet again"—so often placed on the tombstones of loved ones.

And with this Tennyson's immortal hope:

Sunset and evening star,
        And one clear call for me!
And may there be no moaning at the bar,
        When I put out to sea.

But such a tide as moving seems asleep,
    Too full for sound and foam,
When that which drew from out the boundless deep
    Turns home again.

Twilight and evening bell,
    And after that the dark!
And may there be no sadness of farewell,
    When I embark.

For though from out our bourne of Time and Place,
    The flood may bear me far,
I hope to see my Pilot face to face
When I have crossed the bar.

Yes, the life that we have lived here shall go on to fruition over there. The work that we have done faithfully and well here shall be continued there. In the words of Kipling's "L'Envoi":

"When Earth's last picture is painted, and
    the tubes are twisted and dried,
When the oldest colors have faded, and the
    youngest critic has died,
We shall rest, and, faith, we shall need it—
    lie down for an aeon or two,
Till the Master of All Good Workmen shall
    set us to work anew!

"And only the Master shall praise us, and
    only the Master shall blame;
And no one shall work for money, and
    no one shall work for fame;
But each for the joy of working, and
    each, in his separate star,
Shall draw the Thing as he sees it
    for the God of Things as they are!"

The Intermediate State

III. The Intermediate State

1. Nature and Purpose of the Intermediate State

By the intermediate state is meant that realm or condition in which souls exist between death and the resurrection. That there is such a state is acknowledged by practically all who believe in a resurrection and final judgment. The differences of opinion that exist have to do primarily with the nature of the state, — chiefly in controversy with the Roman Catholics, as to whether or not it is purgatorial in character; and with those who, as Jehovah's Witnesses and the Seventh-day Adventists, believe in soul sleep between death and the resurrection; also to some extent with those who believe in a second chance or the possibility of repentance after death.

The doctrine commonly held by the Jews and by the early medieval Church was that believers after death were in a dreamy, semi-conscious state, neither happy nor miserable, awaiting the resurrection of the body. It was in fact not until the Council of Florence, in the year 1439, that the Latin Church expressed outright opposition to this view, and even then it continued to be the prevailing view in the Greek Church.

The Bible has comparatively little to say about the intermediate state, evidently because it is not the ultimate state. It focuses attention not on that which is passing and temporary, but rather on the return of Christ and the new era that shall then begin. We therefore find it difficult to form any adequate idea of the activities that characterize those in the intermediate state.

There are, however, several Scripture passages which teach that it is a state of conscious existence for both the

91

righteous and the wicked, — for the righteous, a state of joy; for the wicked, a state of suffering. This comes out with special clearness in the parable of the rich man and Lazarus, where Lazarus is received into Abraham's bosom, and the rich man is tormented in the flames of hell. Paul's statements already cited (II Cor. 5:8 and Phil. 1:23) make it clear that the state of the believer immediately after death is much to be preferred to the present world. While on the cross Christ said to the dying thief, "Today shalt thou be with me in Paradise," Luke 23:43. For the believer to be in the intermediate state is to be with Christ in Paradise. And Paul's reference to the vision given him early in his ministry, in which in one instance he says that he was "caught up even to the third heaven," and in another that he was "caught up into Paradise," II Cor. 12:2-4, shows that Paradise is to be identified with heaven. And in Rev. 14:13 is found one of the clearest of all references to those in the intermediate state: "Blessed are the dead who die in the Lord from henceforth: yea, saith the Spirit, that they may rest from their labors; for their works follow with them."

The intermediate state is a state of rest and happiness. That, however, does not mean that life there, or life in heaven, will be characterized by idleness and inactivity. Far from it. In the first place, "rest," in Scriptural language, carries with it the idea of *satisfaction in labor,* or *joy in accomplishment.* Even in this world we often find rest in a change in the kind of work we are doing. The activity of the saints is no longer "toil" or "labor," in the sense that it is irksome and tiresome. In this world man in his fallen condition is under sentence to earn his bread by the sweat of his face (Gen. 3:19). Much of his work is misdirected, monotonous, repetitious and vain. But there all of the unpleasant features are removed and it is given a new direction, with new motives, and is a joy to perform. It is no longer directed primarily toward ourselves, nor toward any creature, but toward God. The heavenly life is

one of uninterrupted progress, always upward and onward. The saints are "before the throne of God; and they
serve him day and night in his temple," Rev. 7:15, — they
serve Him in work as well as in worship, His temple perhaps including the entire created universe.

In the second place "rest," in Scriptural language, carries with it the idea of freedom from all that is evil, —
from the temptations and assaults of the evil one, and from
all the allurements of the world which so often have deceived even the Lord's people and caused them to stumble.
Undoubtedly Satan is responsible for much more of our
trouble than we are aware of. Not until we find ourselves
for the first time in a realm where he cannot reach will we
realize how many temptations and troubles were due to his
assaults. This rest consists further in freedom from the
outward cares and sorrows of life, and from the vexations
and perplexities of earthly affairs.

At death the Christian drops entirely out of the world
of sense, and shall belong to it no more until the day of
resurrection, at which time he shall find that the world of
sense also has been "delivered from the bondage of corruption into the liberty of the children of God," Rom.
8:21-23. He is no longer saddened and wearied at heart
by the injustices, violence, opposition and ill-will of evil
men. There is no more pain nor sorrow. "They shall hun-
ger no more, neither thirst any more . . . and God shall wipe
away every tear from their eyes," Rev. 7:16,17. From all
these things the righteous have eternal rest.

The saints from righteous Abel onward, who have passed
from human touch and mortal eyes, live gloriously in the
intermediate state amid the transcendant splendor of Paradise. What it will mean to be with Christ, the incarnate
Son of God, our intimate friend and Elder Brother who
loved us so much that He died for us upon the cross and
who, now glorified, is in the full possession of that glory
which He had with the Father before the world was, is more
than we can comprehend. His prayer was, "Father, I desire

that they also whom thou hast given me be with me where
I am, that they may behold my glory, which thou hast
given me," John 17:24. If the brief transfiguration vision
of Jesus glorified, as seen only through human eyes, was
such as to cause Peter to exclaim, "Lord, it is good for us to
be here," and to cause him to desire to build three taber-
nacles so that the experience might be prolonged (Matt.
17:4), what must it be to be with the glorified Lord in Paradise!

The Scriptures teach that the state into which the righteous enter at death is one of consciousness, holiness and
happiness, which the resurrection and judgment only aug-
ment and make permanent.   The mind loses none of its
power or knowledge at the death of the body. On the contrary, it enters on a much higher plane of existence.   The
first and immediate result is that the soul, freed from the
limitations of earth and cleansed of the last vestiges of sin,
finds its mental and spiritual faculties heightened and is
more alive and active than it ever was before.

The very nature of a finite soul, created in the image of
God, is that it is capable of limitless development. "Image"
means likeness. Man is like God, and different from all the
rest of the creation, in that he is: (1) a thinking, intelligent being; (2) a moral being, having the sense of right
and wrong; (3) holy, as he was originally created and as
he shall be when redemption is complete; (4) immortal, in
that he possesses a soul that shall live for ever; and (5) a
ruler over the lower creation, — he was commanded not
only to dress and keep the garden, but to "subdue" the
earth (Gen. 1:28; 2:15), that is, search out and learn how
to employ for his own use the materials of earth and the
forces of nature. Consequently, man shall continue to grow
in knowledge and wisdom and to gather strength, not only
during the present life and the intermediate state but
through all eternity.

In the present life growth in holiness and intellect is at
best slow and halting. But after death conditions shall be

incomparably more favorable. What marvelous possibilities for the growth of the soul open up during those blessed, peaceful, happy years in immediate fellowship with Christ Himself! The intermediate state is therefore, preeminently a state of special training and education for the high service of the eternal, perfect kingdom. At that time the Lord's people are to be made rulers "over many things," according to His promise, Matt. 25:21,23.

Those who already have passed on and are in the intermediate state doubtless continue to know about affairs in this world, possibly by direct vision, possibly through revelation from God or the angels, or through those who have departed this life later than they. If in this world we have such efficient communication through the purely mechanical means of telephone, radio and television that events in any part of the world can be seen and heard immediately in any other part, need we doubt that in the higher realm communication will be much more direct and efficient than anything that we have known here?

It must be kept in mind that the intermediate state, while a state of freedom from sin and pain and a time of great personal advancement, is, nevertheless, in other respects a state of imperfection. This imperfection consists, first of all, in that the spirit is without a body, which for the human species is an abnormal condition. The body, with its organs of sense, is the instrument through which we make contact with the physical world. As long as the disembodied state continues the soul has, so far as we know, no instrument by which it can make contact with the physical world or communicate with individuals here. The imperfection consists further in the fact that not at death, nor at any time during this present dispensation, is the promised reward given to the Lord's people. It is not the death of the believer, but the second coming of Christ, that is set forth as the time for the distribution of rewards for the labors and self-denials of this life. Paul says that there is laid up for him "the crown of righteousness which the Lord, the righteous judge, shall give to me at that day; and not to me only, but also to all them that have loved his appearing," II Tim. 4:8. So Paul has not yet received his crown, "that day" having not yet come. For that day Paul and all the saints in Paradise are still waiting. Our Lord also taught this same truth when He said of those who when they make a feast, invite the poor and needy, that they "shall be recompensed in the resurrection of the just," Luke 14:12-14. In not a single instance does the Bible connect the bestowal of the promised reward with the death of the believer. The blessings received in the intermediate state, great as they may be, are to be regarded only as an earnest and foretaste of the good things to come.

The life of man thus falls not into two stages, as is so often assumed, but into three. First, there is the stage from birth until death, which is life in the present world and in the natural body; second, life between death and the resurrection, in the intermediate state, which is life without the body; and, third, life in the resurrection body, which is the final and eternal state.

On the other hand the wicked at their death enter immediately into a state of conscious suffering which is heightened and made permanent by the resurrection and judgment. There are not many passages in the Bible that give information concerning the wicked in the intermediate state. The clearest is the parable of the rich man and Lazarus, already referred to. It is interesting to notice that in that parable the rich man was more keenly conscious of the after life than is a normal person in this life, for he knew what was going on in three realms, — his own, that in which Abraham and Lazarus were, which he saw by direct vision, and this world in which his five brothers still were. He had the same character in the other world that he had in this life. There was no break in memory, nor any change in personality. What a man is in this world he remains in the next. It should be observed, of course, that the rich man went to hell not because he was rich, but because he was selfish and hard-hearted, as is shown by the fact that with all his great surplus of goods and possessions he allowed the poor man Lazarus to starve to death at his gate; and Lazarus went to heaven not because he was a poor man but because he was a good man. The rich man lived in separation from God in this life; he could not but live in separation from Him in the next.

This general teaching is briefly summed up in the Westminster Shorter Catechism and in the Westminster Confession of Faith. In answer to the question, "What benefits do believers receive from Christ at death?" the Catechism answers: "The souls of believers are at their death made perfect in holiness and do immediately pass into glory; and their bodies, being still united to Christ, do rest in their graves, till the resurrection."

The Westminster Confession makes a clear statement concerning both the righteous and the wicked when it says that at death, "The souls of the righteous, being then made perfect in holiness, are received into the highest heavens, where they behold the face of God in light and glory, waiting for the full redemption of their bodies; and the souls of the wicked are cast into hell, where they remain in torments and utter darkness, reserved to the judgment of the great day. Besides these two places for souls departed from their bodies, the Scripture acknowledgeth none." (Ch. 32; Sec. 1).

2. Terms: Sheol — Hades

In the Old Testament the Hebrew word used to designate the place of the souls of the dead is *Sheol,* and in the New Testament the equivalent Greek word is *Hades.* There has been much controversy over the precise meaning of these words, and even today there remains a considerable difference of opinion particularly between liberal and conservative scholars.

Let us consider first the word *Sheol.* It is in itself a neutral term, indicating neither happiness nor misery. Frequently it means the grave, or death in the broad sense. It is used in this sense when Jacob, mourning for his son Joseph who he thought had been killed by wild beasts, said: "I will go down to Sheol to my son mourning," Gen. 37:35; and again when Jacob, fearful lest harm should befall Benjamin if he were taken to Egypt by his brothers, said: "If harm befall him by the way in which ye go, then will ye bring down my gray hairs with sorrow to Sheol," Gen. 42:38.

Both the righteous and the wicked are spoken of as descending into Sheol. Concerning the righteous the Psalmist says: "What man is he that shall live and not see death, That shall deliver his soul from the power of Sheol?" Ps. 89:48, and again: "For my soul is full of trouble, And my life draweth nigh unto Sheol," Ps. 88:3. God speaking through the prophet Hosea said: "I will ransom them from the power of Sheol; I will redeem them from death: O death, where are thy plagues? O Sheol, where is thy destruction?" 13:14. As for the wicked, it is said regarding Korah and those associated with him: "So they, and all that appertained unto them, went down alive into Sheol: and the earth closed upon them, and they perished from among the assembly," Nu. 16:33; and again concerning the wicked: "They are appointed as a flock for Sheol; Death shall be their shepherd; And the upright shall have dominion over them in the morning; And their beauty shall be for Sheol to consume," Ps. 49:14.

Several places in the Old Testament descent into Sheol is set forth as a punishment against the wicked: "They spend their days in prosperity, And in a moment they go down to Sheol," Job 21:13; "The wicked shall be turned back unto Sheol, Even all the nations that forget God," Ps. 9:17. In warning against the strange woman Proverbs 7:27 says: "Her house is the way of Sheol, Going down to the chambers of death." God's anger is said to burn there: "For a fire is kindled in mine anger, And burneth unto the lowest Sheol," Deut. 32:22.

On the other hand the Old Testament, as well as the New, represents the state of death for the righteous as one of reward and happiness, and since both the righteous and the wicked go to Sheol the word does not necessarily carry with it either the idea of reward or punishment. Concerning the righteous it is said: "Let me die the death of the righteous, And let my last end be like his," Nu. 23:10; "Thou wilt show me the path of life: In thy presence is fulness of joy; In thy right hand there are pleasures for evermore," Ps. 16:11; and "Thou wilt guide me with thy counsel, And afterward receive me to glory," Ps. 73:24.

Sometimes Sheol is used to designate what we have in mind when we speak of "the unseen world," a disembodied but not an unconscious state of being. Also, in describing the dead, the Scriptures often speak of them as they appear to us, — as in a state of rest, with all of their earthly interests and activities ended. It is in this sense that the term is used in Eccl. 9:10: "Whatsoever thy hand findeth to do, do it with thy might; for there is no work, nor devices, nor knowledge, nor wisdom, in Sheol, whither thou goest."

The view of present day liberal theology is that the Sheol of the Old Testament was a place without moral distinctions, and therefore without blessedness on the one hand, or positive pain on the other. It was, according to this view, a dreamy sort of under-world of comparative inaction, darkness and silence. In opposition to this view Dr. Berkhof says: "The idea is quite prevalent at present that the Old Testament conception of *sheol*, to which that of *hades* in the New Testament is supposed to correspond, was borrowed from the Gentile notion of the underworld. It is held that according to the Old Testament and the New, both the pious and the wicked at death enter the dreamy abode of shades, the land of forgetfulness, where they are doomed to an existence that is merely a dreamy reflection of life on earth. The underworld is in itself neither a place of rewards nor a place of punishment. It is not divided

into different compartments for the good and the bad, but
is a region without moral distinctions. It is a place of weak-
ened consciousness and of slumbrous inactivity, where life
has lost its interests and the joy of life is turned into sadness. Some are of the opinion that the Old Testament represents *sheol* as the permanent abode of all men, while
others find that it holds out a hope of escape for the
pious."[16]   That the liberal view of a dreamy underworld
has little Scriptural support and that it is in fact contrary
to the general Scriptural representations is clear from
what has already been shown.

The word *Hell* never occurs in the Old Testament original
manuscripts.   There are, however, 31 instances in which
the King James Version so translates the word *Sheol*, but
in each instance it is a mistranslation.   There are also 31
instances in which that version translates the word as "the
grave," and 3 in which it is translated as "the pit," although there are entirely different words in the original
for these terms.   The American Standard Version has cor-
rected all of these, uniformly using the untranslated Hebrew word *Sheol*.

In the New Testament the place of the souls of the dead
is usually called *Hades,* although, like the word *Sheol*, this
word is not always used in the same sense.   Sometimes it
means the state of death or disembodied existence.   In this
sense even the soul of Jesus is said to have been in Hades.
In Acts 2:31 Peter says: "Neither was he left in Hades,
nor did his flesh see corruption," — that is, He did not remain in the state of death, nor under the power of death,
but arose in the resurrection.   Historically, the statement
in the Apostles' Creed, "He descended into hell," simply
means that He died, or that He went into the unseen world.

In the following New Testament references the terms
Hades, and Hell (Greek, *Gehenna*), carry with them the
idea of punishment: "And in Hades he lifted up his eyes,

---

16. *Op. cit.*, p. 681.

being in torments," Luke 16:23; "And thou, Capernaum, shalt thou be exalted unto heaven? thou shalt be brought down unto Hades," Matt. 11:23; "Whosoever shall say, Thou fool, shall be in danger of the hell of fire," Matt. 5:22; "Ye offspring of vipers, how shall ye escape the judgment of hell?" Matt. 23:33; etc.

Briefly, we may say that in the Old Testament Sheol usually means the grave, but sometimes the place of punishment, while in the New Testament Hades and Hell usually mean the place of punishment but sometimes the grave.

We may say, therefore, that these words, Sheol and Hades, quite clearly are not always used in the same sense, and that, consequently, they cannot always be translated in the same way, whether it be the state of death, the grave, the place of departed souls, hell, or the underworld. Many of the best scholars, including Vos and Berkhof, maintain that the words do not always have the same meaning.

Furthermore, in this connection something should be said concerning the terms *Paradise* and *Heaven*, and also *Limbus Patrum* and *Limbus Infantum*.

The word *Paradise* is an oriental term, meaning parks or pleasure gardens, and occurs only three times in the entire New Testament. These references are: Luke 23:43, "Today shalt thou be with me in Paradise," — the words of Jesus to the penitent thief; II Cor. 12:4, where Paul says concerning himself that he "was caught up into Paradise, and heard unspeakable words, which it is not lawful for man to utter," which he explains by saying that he was caught up to the third heaven (vs. 3); and Rev. 2:7, "To him that overcometh, to him will I give to eat of the tree of life, which is in the Paradise of God."

These verses make it clear that Paradise is Heaven. It is the place where Christ now is, the place where He manifests His presence and glory. It is sometimes said that, for the redeemed, Paradise is heaven without the body, or that it is heaven before the resurrection. Where Christ's resurrection body is, Heaven is. And since His resurrection body is finite and limited, as is all human nature, that is, not everywhere present but present only in one particular place, Heaven must be a place as well as a state, a place where the saints are exalted and as happy as it is possible for them to be in their present state of existence.

Limbus Patrum. Roman Catholic theology holds that Old Testament believers at their death were gathered into a region called the *limbus patrum*, where they remained without the beatific vision of God, and yet without suffering, until Christ had accomplished His work of redemption. The word *limbus* is from the Latin, meaning fringe or outskirts, and the *limbus patrum* was one of the several compartments into which first Jewish theology and then later Medieval theology divided the unseen world. After His death on the cross, and while His body remained in the grave, Christ is supposed to have descended to this region, delivered the souls held captive there, and led them in triumph to heaven.

This view is derived from I Peter 3:18-20, which passage reads as follows: "Because Christ also suffered for sins once, the righteous for the unrighteous, that he might bring us to God; being put to death in the flesh, but made alive in the spirit; in which also he went and preached unto the spirits in prison, that aforetime were disobedient, when the longsuffering of God waited in the days of Noah, while the ark was a preparing, wherein few, that is, eight souls, were saved through water."

This is admittedly a difficult passage. However, it is capable of quite a different interpretation, and it is therefore a precarious passage on which to build a doctrine. Indeed, some rather fantastic theories have been offered as to what it is intended to teach. We believe, however, that the correct interpretation is not too difficult to find. Let us keep in mind that throughout Christ's earthly career His obedience to the will of the Father was accomplished through the leading and motivation of the Holy Spirit. The Holy Spirit came upon the virgin Mary before He was born,

Luke 1:35; the Spirit descended in a visible form at the time of His baptism, Matt. 3:16; and following the baptism He was led of the Spirit into the wilderness where He was forty days and forty nights, Matt: 4:1. Throughout His entire earthly career He was obedient to the will of the Father, and the way in which that obedience was accomplished was by the leading, the motive power, the anointing of the Holy Spirit. I Peter 3:18 says that after His crucifixion He was "made alive in the Spirit." This, we believe, means the Holy Spirit. Verse 19 tells us that it was in this same Spirit that "he went and preached unto the spirits in prison, that aforetime were disobedient." And when did the Spirit of Christ preach to those spirits? Verse 20 tells us: "When the longsuffering of God waited in the days of Noah, while the ark was a preparing, wherein few, that is, eight souls, were saved through water." In other words, it was the same Spirit of Christ who spoke through Noah to the people of his day. The preaching referred to by Peter was long since past. It occurred while the ark was in process of construction; and the tragic thing about it is that only eight souls responded to that preaching. Those eight, and only those, were saved through water. Those who refused the testimony of the Spirit of Christ as He spoke through Noah were "the spirits in prison," that is, in the prison house of sin, or in hell, at the time Peter wrote, and they still are imprisoned. There is, therefore, no foundation here for the doctrine of a "limbus patrum." It needs only to be said further, however, that according to Roman Catholic theology this region is now empty.

Limbus Infantum. Roman Catholic theology also holds that all unbaptized infants, whether of heathen or Christian parents, are excluded from heaven and are confined to a region known as the "limbus infantum." This doctrine is founded on John 3:5, "Except one be born of water and the Spirit, he cannot enter into the kingdom of God," which is interpreted to mean that no unbaptized person, child or adult, can be saved. This is closely connected with their

doctrine of baptismal regeneration, which holds that the
soul is spiritually renewed at the time of baptism and that
all persons dying unbaptized carry with them the guilt of
original sin. The ecumenical councils of Lyons and Florence and the canons of the Council of Trent (1563) declare
very positively that the souls of unbaptized infants are confined to this realm; but the Roman Catholic Church has
never defined the nature of the punishment except to say
that they are not saved. There has always been a natural
repugnance to the idea that these children are lost, and
Roman Catholic theologians have differed considerably as
to their condition, with probably the majority holding that
they endure no positive suffering but only are excluded
from the blessings of Heaven. What a contrast is all of this
with the generally accepted Protestant doctrine that all of
those dying in infancy are saved!

3. Second Probation

The theory of "second probation" or "second chance"
holds that those who die unsaved have another chance for
salvation in the next life. Almost universally the Christian
Church has held that only those who are believers at death
are saved, and that there is no second chance nor opportunity of any kind for repentance after death. The opposite view has been held only by individuals or by comparatively small groups. In the early ages only Origen and a
few mystics held that view. At the time of the Reformation some of the Anabaptists held that a second chance was
given. During the nineteenth century several theologians
in Germany and England, most prominent of whom was
Schliermacher in Germany, embraced the idea and gave a
considerable impulse to that kind of teaching. In more
recent times the sect known as Jehovah's witnesses began
to propagate it aggressively. As Modernism, with its more
or less consistent denial of the supernatural all through the
Christian system, has become more prominent the doctrine
of a second probation has become much more popular. It

has been made the distinctive tenet of the Universalists. (The Roman Catholic doctrine of Purgatory, as it bears on this subject, will be discussed in a later chapter).

Opinions vary among those who believe in a second probation as to whether this opportunity is offered to all or only to certain classes. Practically all agree that the offer is made to all those who die in infancy and to all adult heathen who in this life did not hear the Gospel, and the general tendency is to extend it also to those who never seriously considered the claims of Christ or who rejected Him. Most of those holding this view say that none are condemned except those who obstinately resist. Some hold that the unsaved undergo a new period of training, and that this training may be so prolonged and intensified that eventually every human being is brought to salvation. This latter, of course, is Universalism. It makes the pains suffered after death to be primarily disciplinary in character rather than punitive and vindicatory.

Support for the theory of second probation is based more on general humanitarian conjectures or surmises of what God in His love and goodness might be expected to do, and on an easily understood desire to extend the atonement as far as possible, rather than on any solid Scriptural foundation. The Scripture on which advocates of this view rely primarily is I Peter 3:18-20, holding that Christ, between the time of His death and resurrection, went to the underworld and preached to the spirits of those who had died before His crucifixion, offering them salvation through the atonement that had just been provided. In the preceding section we have given what we believe to be the correct interpretation of those verses. If that interpretation is correct, they have no bearing at all on the subject of second probation. In any event they could apply only to those who had died before the time of the crucifixion. Those who have died since, particularly those who have heard the Gospel and rejected it, have had much fuller opportunity and ap-

parently would be dealt with in a different manner. But
on the basis of strict exegesis those verses give no support
to the theory that those who refuse the testimony of God
in grace in this world have the Gospel preached to them in
a future probation. The solemn reality is that all who die
in unbelief pass beyond death to a lost eternity. There is
nothing in Scripture to indicate that they receive a second
chance.

Scripture uniformly represents the state of the righteous and that of the wicked after death as fixed. Perhaps
the most important passage in this connection is the parable of the rich man and Lazarus, Luke 16:19-31. "Between us and you," said Abraham, "there is a great gulf
fixed, that they that would pass from hence to you may not
be able, and that none may pass over from thence to us."
Jesus gave the stern warning, "Except ye believe that I am
he, ye shall die in your sins," John 8:24. On four different
occasions He declared that after the rejection of the opportunity afforded in this life "there shall be the weeping
and the gnashing of teeth," — Matt. 13:42, the parable of
the tares; Matt. 22:13, the parable of the wedding feast
and the slighted invitations; Matt. 24:51, the parable of
the unfaithful servant; and Matt. 25:30, the parable of the
talents. This hard saying obviously indicates absolute
misery in a permanent condition, and His repeated use of
it shows His concern that it be deeply impressed upon our
minds. It shows further that He was aware of the inclination among men to soften the absolute antithesis between
salvation and an eternally lost spiritual condition.

The theory of second probation is refuted by those passages in which death is represented as the decisive time
for which man must watch and be ready. One of the most
striking verses is Heb. 9:27: "It is appointed unto men
once to die, and after this cometh judgment." Here the end
of this life and the final judgment are brought into immediate connection, as if there were no intermediate state at

all. In II Cor. 5:10 Paul says: "For we must all be made manifest before the judgment seat of Christ; that each one may receive the things done in the body, according to what he hath done, whether it be good or bad." "Behold, *now* is the acceptable time; behold *now* is the day of salvation," II Cor. 6:2.

There is not one verse in Scripture that lends any real support to the idea of a second probation. Its consistent teaching rather is that it is in this world that man's fate for good or evil is decided, that what the person is at death he continues to be throughout all eternity. Once man has passed the boundaries of this life there is no turning back, no recall. A great and impassible gulf separates the righteous from the wicked, and the intermediate state is of no value whatever in preparing for the judgment.

The theory of second probation rests on the assumption that only the conscious, deliberate rejection of Christ and His Gospel is sufficient to condemn man. Unbelief is, of course, a great sin; but it is not the only form of revolt against God, nor the only ground for condemnation. Man is in a lost condition as a result of the fall of the race in Adam. Until he is regenerated and converted he is a victim of original sin as well as of actual or personal sin. Original sin is in itself sufficient to bring a person into condemnation, although his penalty would not be as severe as if actual sin were added. The Baptist theologian, Dr. Augustus H. Strong, has pointed this out quite clearly in the following paragraph:

"The theory of second probation is in part a consequence of denying the old orthodox and Pauline doctrine of the organic unity of the race in Adam's first transgression. Liberal theology has been inclined to deride the notion of a fair probation of humanity in our first father, and of a common sin and guilt of mankind in him. It cannot find what is regarded as a fair probation for each individual since that first sin; and the conclusion is easy that there must be such a fair probation for each individual in the world to come. But we may advise those who take this view to return to the old theology. Grant a fair probation of the whole race already passed, and the condition of mankind is no longer that of mere unfortunates unjustly circumstanced, but rather that of beings guilty and condemned, to whom present opportunity, and even present existence, is a matter of pure grace, — and much more is the general provision of salvation and the offer of it to any human soul a matter of pure grace. The world is already a place of second probation; and since the second probation is due wholly to God's mercy, no probation after death is needed to vindicate the justice or goodness of God."[17]

A further serious objection to the theory of a future probation is that it depreciates the importance of the present life and well nigh extinguishes missionary zeal. If there is to be a future probation, or perhaps a series of future probations until all are saved, it is at least of lesser importance whether or not we get right with God in this present life, and whether or not we carry the message to those who have not heard it. Certainly the need for any one to repent now is not so urgent if he is to have another chance later on. The traditional Christian view has been that we must evangelize all men everywhere or they perish. The practical effect of this theory if widely adopted would be to lower the moral tone at home and to discourage foreign missions.

4. Soul Sleep

The doctrine of soul sleep holds that the soul becomes unconscious at death and that it continues in that condition until the resurrection. According to this doctrine the souls of the dead are sleeping in the grave, that is, in a silent world in which there is no knowledge, consciousness or activity.

---

17. *Systematic Theology*, p. 1043.

Doubtless the idea of soul sleep has arisen in part from the appearance of the body after death, which condition resembles that of physical sleep. The body is ordinarily placed in a recumbent position, and particularly among Christians it is cared for with a special sense of love and tenderness, similar to putting a child to bed for rest in sleep. The dead body and the body asleep are so much alike in appearance that it becomes a natural thing to speak of death as an unending sleep. Even those who are firm believers in the continued conscious activity of the soul after death often speak of it in this manner. And similarly the Bible, as was said earlier, sometimes describes things as they appear rather than as they are actually known to be.

This doctrine is one of the distinctive tenets of Jehovah's Witnesses, and also of the Seventh-day Adventists. Historically it has been held only by small isolated groups, and has always been opposed by the main body of the Christian Church. In this connection Prof. Berkhof says: "Eusebius makes mention of a small sect in Arabia that held this view. During the Middle Ages there were quite a few so-called Psychopannychians, and at the time of the Reformation this error was advocated by some of the Anabaptists. Calvin even wrote a treatise against them under the title *Psychopannychia*. In the nineteenth century this doctrine was held by some of the Irvingites in England, and in our day it is one of the favorite doctrines of the Russellites or Millennial Dawnists of our own country. According to the latter, body and soul descend into the grave, the soul in a state of sleep, which really amounts to a state of nonexistence. What is called the resurrection is in reality a new creation. During the Millennium the wicked will have a second chance, but if they show no marked improvement during the first hundred years, they will be annihilated. If in that period they give evidence of some amendment of life, their probation will continue, but only to end in annihilation, if they remain impenitent. There is no hell, no place of eternal torment."[18]

Seventh-day Adventists illustrate their doctrine by comparison with what happens when the light bulb is loosened in the socket so that the current is broken. The light goes out. It stays out until the bulb is re-connected with the current. Then it again gives light. Says one writer: "A man's light, or life, goes out at death, and he does not live again until the resurrection." Jehovah's Witnesses are equally insistent that man's life ceases completely between death and the resurrection.

But the fallacy of this argument is that it assumes the very thing that is to be proved, which is, that the soul, like the light, ceases to exist at death. No proof is offered for that assumption, except that we no longer see it. The fact is that the two cases are quite different. It is not the *same* light that comes back into existence when the current is again contacted, but entirely new light, which is continuously re-created. On the other hand, the soul of man is a continuing, abiding reality. The soul that is rewarded in heaven or punished in hell is the *same* soul that lived on earth. If that soul ceased to exist at death, and a new soul were created at the resurrection, it could not possibly be the same soul, and could not justly be rewarded or punished for what the former soul has done. If as has been said of the disembodied soul, "its light, or life, goes out at death," it cannot possibly be the same soul that is brought back into existence at the resurrection. This becomes quite clear when we remember that a soul apart from a body is simply a spirit, a conscious life. The essential characteristic of a spirit is life. It has no material substance in which its identity can be carried. There can be no such thing as a non-living spirit, for the reason that consciousness, or life, is the thing which constitutes it a spirit.

---

18. *Op. cit.*, p. 688.

In opposition to the doctrine of soul sleep we insist that death is not extinction, but only the separation of the soul from the body. The soul continues to exist, fully conscious and active, and at the resurrection this same soul, not a new one, is reunited with the body. We may well ask, How can a non-existent person be brought back into existence? In what sense would this person be the same person who formerly lived? And as regards the wicked we may ask, Why should non-existent sinners be brought back into existence at all? Or why should they be brought back into existence only for the purpose of putting them out of existence a second time?

The main Scripture references relied on by those who teach soul sleep are the following:

(1) From the New Testament: "Our friend Lazarus is fallen asleep; but I go, that I may wake him out of sleep. . . . Then Jesus therefore said unto them plainly, Lazarus is dead," John 11:11-14. Concerning the ruler's daughter who had died Jesus said, "The damsel is not dead, but sleepeth," Matt. 9:24. The first martyr, Stephen, died as a result of being stoned, and we are told that "he fell asleep," Acts 7:60. Paul uses this expression on several occasions. "Behold, I tell you a mystery: We shall not all sleep, but we shall all be changed," I Cor. 15:51. "But we would not have you ignorant, brethren, concerning them that fall asleep; that ye sorrow not, even as the rest, who have no hope. For if we believe that Jesus died and rose again, even so them also that are fallen asleep in Jesus will God bring with him," I Thess. 4:13,14.

(2) From the Old Testament: "For the living know that they shall die: but the dead know not anything, neither have they any more reward; for the memory of them is forgotten. As well their love, as their hatred and their envy, is perished long ago; neither have they any more a portion for ever in anything that is done under the sun," Eccl. 9:5,6. "Whatsoever thy hand findeth to do, do it with thy might; for there is no work, nor device, nor

knowledge, nor wisdom in Sheol, whither thou goest," Eccl.
9:10. "Consider and answer me, O Jehovah my God:
Lighten mine eyes, lest I sleep the sleep of death," Ps. 13:3.
"For in death there is no remembrance of thee: In Sheol
who shall give thee thanks?" Ps. 6:5. "The dead praise not
Jehovah, Neither any that go down into silence," Ps.
115:17. "His (man's) breath goeth forth, he returneth to
his earth; In that very day his thoughts perish," Ps.
146:3,4. Daniel refers to "them that sleep in the dust of
the earth," 12:2.

But these verses present no real difficulty. It should be
clear to any one that these verses describe the dead person
only as he appears from the human viewpoint, not as he
really is. The language is that of appearance only. Similarly, the Bible speaks of "the four corners of the earth,"
Rev. 20:8; of "the ends of the earth," Zech. 9:10; of the
sun rising and setting; etc. Outwardly the dead person
does look as if he were "at rest" or "asleep." He can no
longer hear, nor speak, nor move, nor in any way take
part in the activities of this world. But not one of the verses quoted is intended to give a description of the person
or his activities in the next world, nor does any one of
them make any attempt whatever to enter into the reality
that underlies death.

Everyone acknowledges, of course, that the *body* does
sleep until the resurrection, that is, it becomes unconscious,
insensible. The sleep spoken of is that of the body, not of
the soul. Those who teach soul sleep have simply confused
the sleep of the body with that of the soul. Soul sleep is not
taught anywhere in the Bible. In every instance in which
the word sleep is used in connection with the dead the con-
text makes it clear that it applies only to the body.

The parable of the rich man and Lazarus, which tells so
much about the intermediate state and to which we find
it necessary to refer so often, answers this question completely. There we have a picture of both the saved and the
lost immediately after death. Lazarus was in Abraham's

bosom, or Paradise, and the rich man was in hell. Both were fully awake and conscious. Abraham and the rich man recognized each other. They talked back and forth, and remembered the scenes of earth. Lazarus had the feeling of happiness and comfort, while the rich man had the feeling of misery and torment. What could better picture perfect consciousness? Poor consolation it would have been for Lazarus to be in Abraham's bosom if he were unconscious, as some would have us believe, and did not know that he was there!

It will do no good for any one to object that this was only a parable. For the parables spoken by Jesus were true to life and based on realities. The parables of the sower, of the prodigal son, of the vine, fig tree, etc., are given because in real life there are sowers, prodigal sons, vines, fig trees, etc. A parable must give a true picture of the thing it illustrates if it is to be of any service. Otherwise it becomes misleading. Furthermore, these events are spoken of as having taken place during the earth time, that is, before the end of the world. Jesus Himself told the parables. Surely He knew what the realities were, and surely He would not have used words that would have deceived His hearers.

But apart from this parable there is abundant Scripture to prove that believers do enjoy a conscious life in connection with God and with Christ immediately after death. To the penitent thief on the cross Jesus said, "Today shalt thou be with me in Paradise," Luke 23:43. Those words would have afforded little comfort if he were to sink into a state of dead unconsciousness, only to be awakened by the judgment trumpet. Instead of a long unconscious sleep he had the assurance that that day he would be with Christ in Paradise. The spirit of Jesus went immediately to the Father, and with him went the spirit of this poor victim, saved by faith. To transpose the word "today," as the Adventists attempt to do, making the verse read, "Today I say unto thee, thou shalt be with me in Paradise," is char-

acterized by the best exegetical authorities as entirely un-
authorized and as simply forcing the sense of the passage.

At the transfiguration scene, Matt. 17:1-8, Moses and
Elijah appeared and talked with Jesus. They were not
soul-sleeping. Moses had been dead fifteen centuries and
his body had long since mingled with the dust of the earth,
but now he appears, alive and conscious. Elijah, too, had
been taken out of the world centuries earlier. But here he
is, very much alive.

Our Lord, in His argument with the Sadducees, appealed
to the Old Testament to prove that three men, Abraham,
Isaac and Jacob, were then living and enjoying a conscious
life of communion with God: "But that the dead are raised,
even Moses showed, in the place concerning the Bush, when
he calleth the Lord the God of Abraham, and the God of
Isaac, and the God of Jacob. Now he is [present tense]
not the God of the dead, but of the living," Luke 20:37,38.
The bodies of those men were dead, but their spirits were
alive. Let it be kept in mind that the angels, who are pure
spirits entirely apart from any bodies, are not soul-sleeping. Why, then, should it be thought that human souls
must sleep when separate from their bodies? This was the
argument of the Pharisees against their rivals, the materialistic minded Sadducees, namely, that *the existence of
angels proves that spirits can and do live apart from the
body.* The old Sadducees differed from the modern soul
sleepers to this extent: they were more consistent in that
they denied completely any future life, whereas the mod-
erns believe that after a period of unconsciousness the
soul will be brought back to consciousness at the resurrection to be united with the body.

It should be kept in mind that resurrection applies not
to the soul, but only to the *body.* It is not the soul, but
the body, that rises. This is the teaching of the Bible when,
for instance, we are told that at the crucifixion of Jesus
"the tombs were opened; and many bodies of the saints

that had fallen asleep were raised," Matt. 27:52. The soul needs no resurrection, for it does not die.

The dying martyr, Stephen, with the full light of inspiration in his mind, declared that he saw the heavens opened and the Son of man standing on the right hand of God, — standing there, waiting for him (Acts 7:56). So Stephen was not going into a state of soul sleep.

Paul indicates that the Christian at death is immediately present with Christ: "For to me to live is Christ, and to die is gain . . . . But I am in a strait betwixt the two, having the desire to depart and be with Christ; for it is very far better," Phil. 1:21,23. That can only mean that he expected to be conscious in the presence of the Lord and to receive an immediate blessing. Again he says: "Whilst we are at home in the body, we are absent from the Lord. . . willing rather to be absent from the body, and to be at home with the Lord," II Cor. 5:6,8. He certainly would not have spoken after that fashion about an unconscious existence, which is a virtual non-existence. What possible satisfaction could there be in being unconsciously "at home with the Lord?" These words can have no other meaning than that he expected to be conscious immediately after death. With his burning desire to render much-needed service to the newly established churches, he would have preferred to have lived and labored, even amid great sufferings, rather than to have died if death had only meant entering into a state of unconsciousness and inaction. To be at home with the Lord loses all meaning if there is no consciousness.

Again, Paul's teaching is set forth in II Cor. 5:1-3: "For we know that if the earthly house of our tabernacle be dissolved, we have a building from God, a house not made with hands, eternal, in the heavens. For verily in this we groan, longing to be clothed upon with our habitation which is from heaven: if so be that being clothed we shall not be found naked." Here he makes it plain that after death he would know the difference between having a body and not having a body. Having a body is like being "clothed," while being without the body gives a sense of being "naked." The body is likened to a garment to which we have become accustomed and which we miss when it is taken from us. In other words, he makes it clear that after death he expects to know the difference between having a body and being in a disembodied state. An unconscious soul could not know that difference.

These and various other passages teach clearly and forcefully that souls do exist and that they are conscious between death and the resurrection. All of these relate to time before the resurrection. Surely there is no room left for the erroneous doctrine of soul sleeping.

In defense of their position the Adventists say that none of those who were raised from the dead have given any account of their experience, and that this in an indication that they were unconscious while in the disembodied state. But in reply we must point out that that is merely an argument from silence, and in this case quite worthless since Scripture in other places clearly teaches that those in the intermediate state are conscious. It is entirely possible that those who were brought back to life did tell something of their experiences, but that the accounts, like many other events and discourses of that day, were not recorded by the gospel writers. More probable is the explanation that what those persons experienced while in the disembodied state was so unlike anything in this life that it could not be expressed in human language, just as the language of higher mathematics or of chemical formulas is unintelligible to any one who has not studied in those fields. A few years ago when Professor Einstein propounded a new theory in regard to the relation between gravitation and magnetism his thesis was printed by newspapers as a human interest feature; but the peculiar signs and symbols that he used meant absolutely nothing to the vast majority of the people who saw them. This explanation is hinted at, if not clearly taught, by Paul in II Cor. 12:4, where he says that he was "caught up into paradise, and heard unspeakable words, which it is not lawful for man to utter."

In the light of all this evidence we must conclude that the intermediate state is a state of consciousness, recognition and remembrance. There is no reason to believe that at death either the good or the evil enter into a state of abeyance or suspense. The innate activity of the soul would of itself make it probable that the soul would continue conscious and that it would enter upon the preliminary state of its reward or punishment as soon as that is completely earned. Those who teach soul sleep are confusing what is said of the body with what is said of the soul, and are setting forth a doctrine that is contradicted by many Scripture passages.

5. Annihilation

The same two groups that teach soul sleep, Jehovah's Witnesses and the Seventh-day Adventists, as well as a few others, have also taken quite an aggressive stand in asserting that after the final judgment all impenitent souls will be annihilated. And by annihilation is meant a literal cessation of being. This we may call conditional immortality. The form in which this view usually has been held is that man was created mortal, and that immortality is a gift which God confers as a reward upon the righteous, although some have held that man was created immortal but that the wicked are, by a positive act of God, deprived of that gift.

This theory has been brought forward primarily for the purpose of softening down or doing away with the difficulties connected with the doctrine of eternal punishment. Some believers teach it because they think it necessary in order to defend the character of God, so to speak, against the charge of unkindness and cruelty. Some of the wicked affirm it in order to escape the reality of hell. The motives of these latter are personal and selfish. In their case the wish is father to the thought. But the fact of the matter

is that annihilation can hardly be called a punishment, certainly not an adequate punishment, for sin. It implies a
termination of consciousness and therefore of all pain and
all sense of guilt or ill-desert. For many the fear or dread
of annihilation would not in itself be anything like commensurate with the transgression. For those who grow
tired of life, and particularly for those who have an ac-
cusing conscience, extinction of being might be considered
a very desirable thing. For such persons it would in reality be a blessing. This view, like that of second probation
and soul sleep, has always been opposed by the church at
large.

In opposition to this theory the Bible not only gives no
hint of any cessation of the punishment of the wicked but
declares in the strongest terms its endlessness. It is said
to be "eternal," "everlasting." These words are the strongest of any in the Greek language. These same words are
used to express the eternity of God, and to describe the
duration of the blessed condition of the righteous in heaven.
"Now unto the King eternal, immortal, invisible, the only
God, be honor and glory for ever and ever," I Tim. 1:17.
"He that believeth . . . hath eternal life," John 5:24. "I
give unto them eternal life," John 10:28. "The free gift of
God is eternal life in Jesus Christ our Lord," Rom. 6:23.
"Depart from me, ye cursed, into the eternal fire which is
prepared for the Devil and his angels . . . . And these shall
go away into eternal punishment: but the righteous into
eternal life," Matt. 25:41,46. In this latter verse the same
Greek word is used in both clauses. The wicked are to go
"eis kolasin aionion," and the righteous "eis zoen aionion";
hence the meaning must be the same in both cases. The
word "aionion" is used in the New Testament seventy-two
times, and always it denotes indefinite, unbounded, eternal
duration. The judgment scene of Matt. 25:31-46 implies
the continued existence of both the righteous and the
wicked. Blessing is asserted for the one, and punishment

for the other.   The parallel would not hold at all if the wicked were to be annihilated.

The theory of annihilation does violence to the justice of God. Justice demands that the sinner shall receive punishment commensurate with his crime, not annihilation. The Bible teaches that there will be degrees of punishment for the wicked, — some will be beaten with few stripes, and some with many stripes, but in each case the punishment continues for ever. Let it be kept in mind also that with all restraints removed the sinner goes on sinning endlessly, defiantly, against God, and that *endless* punishment is the penalty for *endless* sinning.

That the sufferings of the wicked have no end is taught most unequivocally in the following verses: "And the smoke of their torment goeth up for ever and ever; and they have no rest day and night, they that worship the beast and his image, and whoso receiveth the mark of his name," Rev. 14:11. "And the Devil that deceived them was cast into the lake of fire and brimstone, where are also the beast and the false prophet; and they shall be tormented day and night for ever and ever," Rev. 20:10. ". . . who shall suffer punishment, even eternal destruction from the face of the Lord," II Thess. 1:9. Jude, verse 13, refers to the wicked as "wandering stars, for whom the blackness of darkness hath been reserved for ever"; and in verse 7 the wicked are referred to as "suffering the punishment of eternal fire." In Mark 9:43 we are told that the fire is "unquenchable," and in verse 48 that "their worm dieth not, and the fire is not quenched." Daniel declares that "Many of them that sleep in the dust of the earth shall awake, some to everylasting life, and some to shame and everlasting contempt," 12:2.

In these verses it is not said that the effects of this punishment are everlasting, as would be the case if the wicked were annihilated, but that the punishment itself — the "fire," the "punishment," the "torment," the "contempt," the "worm" — is everlasting. What would be the sense of these being everlasting if the sinner himself had ceased to exist? If these expressions do not teach that the punishment of the wicked continues eternally, it is difficult to see how it could be taught in human language. God does not annihilate the wicked, whether men or angels, but makes them the means of displaying eternally His hatred for sin, as His holiness and justice are manifested in that punishment.

There is a close parallel between the fate of wicked men and lost angels, as we have just seen in Matt. 25:41. In this connection Dr. A. A. Hodge has said, "The demons sinned before Adam fell. Ever since, for many thousand years, they have been 'reserved in everlasting chains under darkness, unto the judgment of the great day' (Jude 6). They are punished for sin, yet have for many thousand years not ceased to exist. Many of them, doing their evil work among men on earth, prove their conscious activity under a state of penalty (Matt. 12:43). No possible language can more explicitly declare that the Devil shall be tormented, kept in conscious suffering, ceaseless and endless. And into the same 'everlasting fire prepared for the Devil,' are wicked men to be sent from the left hand of the judge (Matt. 25:41)."[19]

Rev. Arthur Allen, editor of an Australian church magazine, recently stated the case in these words: "So far as our existence is concerned, we have been created like unto the angels. Satan was an angel that sinned against God, but his sin did not destroy his existence. He lives on and must live on forever. What happened was that his abode and his character were changed, but his being remained the same. Sin has brought a similar change in man. His abode was changed, he was cast out of Eden and from the presence of God. His character was changed from the light of purity to the darkness of corruption, but his being remains the same. The distinctiveness of his individuality re-

19. Pamphlet, *Immortality Not Conditional*, p. 12.

mains, his personality is immortal. He has begun an endless existence and has no choice, but must live on. Christ has revealed this in the case of Lazarus. Dives lived on, his thoughts and personality were unimpaired, from hell he spoke for his brethren, 'that they should not come to this place of torment.' "[20]

When the Bible says that the wicked are to "perish," or to be "destroyed," that does not mean that they are to be reduced to a state of non-existence. These words signify a continued condition of privation or of suffering. A sinner alienated from God is already "lost," "destroyed," "ruined," but he has not ceased to exist. Eternal death is not the extinction of being but of well-being. Dr. Charles Hodge put this clearly when he said:

"The word death, when spoken of the soul, means alienation or separation from God; and when that separation is final it is eternal death. This is so plain that it never has been doubted, except for the purpose of supporting the doctrine of the annihilation of the wicked. The same remark applies to the use of the words 'destroy' and 'perish.' To destroy is to ruin. The nature of the ruin depends on the nature of the subject of which it is predicated. A thing is ruined when it is rendered unfit for use; and when it is in such a state that it can no longer answer the end for which it was designed. A ship at sea, dismantled, rudderless, with its sides battered in, is ruined, but not annihilated. It is a ship still. A man destroys himself when he ruins his health, squanders his property, debases his character, and renders himself unfit to act his part in life. A soul is utterly and forever destroyed when it is reprobated, alienated from God, rendered a fit companion only for the Devil and his angels. This is a destruction a thousandfold more dreadful than mere annihilation."[21]

Jehovah's Witnesses and Seventh-day Adventists teach that eventually all evil is to be abolished. Wicked men and

---

20. *The Australian Free Presbyterian*, Jan. 15, 1947.
21. *Op. cit.*, III, p. 874.

angels, they say, including Satan himself, are to be cast into "the lake of fire," along with the agencies that they have used to accomplish their ends, and all of these are to be completely consumed. When these things are destroyed rebellion comes to an end, and God makes "a new heaven and a new earth." Thus, according to their doctrines, only good eventually will remain, a universe without sin. This view naturally appeals to human sentiment, and we might wish it were true. But the difficulty is that it clearly contradicts what the Bible teaches.

It is said by some of those who teach annihilation that there will be no resurrection of the wicked — another sentimental scheme to which we might readily consent if it were given to us to arrange a universe according to our own liking. But to refute this we need only turn to the following: "For the hour cometh in which all that are in the tombs shall hear his voice, and shall come forth: they that have done good, unto the resurrection of life; and they that have done evil, unto the resurrection of judgment," John 5:28, 29. Paul's words to Felix the governor were: "...there shall be a resurrection both of the just and unjust," Acts 24:15. And Daniel said: "Many of them that sleep in the dust of the earth shall awake, some to everlasting life, and some to shame and everlasting contempt," 12:2.

The annihilationists have only a comparatively small following because there is a consciousness in all men that death does not end all. The idea of immortality is so deeply rooted in the human mind that most unrepentant persons are afraid to die because they are worried, sometimes terrified, by the uncertainty of what lies beyond.

One further point should be brought out in this connection. In defense of their doctrine of annihilation Jehovah's Witnesses and Seventh-day Adventists say that nowhere in the Bible is man said to be immortal, and that God alone is declared to be immortal. As proof they cite I Tim.

6:15,16, which reads, ". . . the King of kings, and Lord of lords; who only hath immortality."

In response to that we acknowledge that in the strictest and highest sense God alone has immortality, in that He alone has existed from eternity and always will exist. He is the only absolute Being. But when human souls are created in His image, while they have a beginning, they have no ending and are from that time on immortal. To be immortal means to be never-dying. Man's body is mortal; but his soul is immortal. In I Cor. 15:53,54 Paul says, "For this corruptible must put on incorruption, and this mortal must put on immortality. But when this corruptible shall have put on incorruption, and this mortal shall have put on immortality, then shall come to pass the saying that is written, Death is swallowed up in victory." Jesus said to Martha, "He that liveth and believeth on me shall never die," John 11:26. The believer never dies spiritually. The unbeliever, like the Devil and the demons, is already dead spiritually, for Paul says, "And you did he make alive, when ye were dead through your trespasses and sins . . . But God . . . even when we were dead through our trespasses, made us alive together with Christ," Eph. 2:1-5. The believer does suffer physical death, which is separation of body and soul, but he does not die spiritually. The unbeliever not only dies physically, but is already dead spiritually and needs first of all to be "born anew," that is, to be regenerated or given a new principle of spiritual life by the Holy Spirit. But while he is dead spiritually, that does not mean that his spirit is inactive or unconscious. Technically, the term "immortal," in the strict sense, is nowhere in Scripture used to describe man, just as the word "Trinity" is nowhere used to describe God. But in each case the underlying truth is clearly there. And, what is more important, while the Scriptures do not apply to man the word "immortal," they do apply to him the word *life*, which has a deeper and richer concept. The righteous have spiritual and eternal life. "Life," in Scriptural and theological

124 IMMORTALITY

language, means not primarily continuation of existence, but a rich spiritual existence in association with God; and likewise "death," in Scriptural and theological language, means primarily not cessation of existence, nor separation of body and spirit, but separation from God.

6. Purgatory

The Roman Catholic Church has built up a doctrine in which it is held that all who die at peace with the Church, but who are not perfect, must undergo penal and purifying suffering in an intermediate realm known as purgatory. Only those believers who have attained a state of Christian perfection go immediately to heaven. All unbaptized adults and those who after baptism have committed mortal sin go immediately to hell. The great mass of partially sanctified Christians dying in fellowship with the Church, but who nevertheless are encumbered with some degree of sin, go to purgatory where, for a longer or shorter time they suffer until all sin is purged away, after which they are translated to heaven.

The Roman Church holds that baptism removes all previous guilt, both original and actual, so that if a person were to die immediately thereafter he would go directly to heaven. All other believers, except the Christian martyrs but including even the highest clergy, must go to purgatory to pay the penalty for sins committed after baptism. The sacrifices made by the martyrs, particularly as those sufferings reflect honor upon the Church, are considered an adequate substitute for the purgatorial sufferings.

The sufferings in purgatory are said to vary greatly in intensity and duration, being proportioned in general to the guilt and impurity or impenitence of the sufferer. They are described as being in some cases comparatively light and mild, lasting perhaps only a few hours, while in others little if anything short of the torments of hell itself and

lasting for thousands of years. They differ from the pains
of hell at least to this extent, that there is a limit to the
former but not to the latter. They are, in any event, to end
with the last judgment. Hence purgatory, like the Limbus
Patrum, eventually is to be emptied of all its victims.

As regards the intensity of the suffering, Bellarmine, a
noted Roman Catholic theologian, says: "The pains of
purgatory are very severe, surpassing anything endured
in this life." The Manual of the Purgatorial Society, established in 1930 with the imprimatur of Cardinal Hayes,
says: "According to the Holy Fathers of the Church, the
fire of purgatory does not differ from the fire of hell, except in point of duration. 'It is the same fire,' says St.
Thomas Aquinas, 'that torments the reprobates in hell,
and the just in purgatory. The least pain in purgatory,'
he says, 'surpasses the greatest sufferings in this life.'
Nothing but the eternal duration makes the fire of hell
more terrible than that of purgatory."

It seems that the Church of Rome has rather wisely ab-
stained from any official pronouncements concerning the
nature and intensity of purgatorial suffering. Books and
literature intended for Protestant readers or hearers speak
of it only in the mildest terms. But the Church does not
thereby escape responsibility, for it has always allowed
free circulation, with its expressed or implied sanction, of
books containing the most frightening descriptions, rang-
ing all the way from comparatively mild disciplinary measures to a burning lake of billowing flames in which the
souls of the impenitent are submerged. Among their own
people and in the hands of the priests it has been an instrument of terrifying power. We are reminded of the remark of Charles Hodge in this connection: "The feet of
the tiger with its claws withdrawn are as soft as velvet;
but when those claws are extended, they are fearful instruments of laceration and death."

In general it is held by the Roman Catholic Church that
the period of suffering in purgatory can be shortened by

gifts of money, prayers by the priests, and masses, which gifts, prayers and masses can be provided for by the person before death or by relatives and friends after death. Purgatory is supposed to be under the special jurisdiction of the Pope, and· it is his prerogative as the representative of Christ on earth to grant indulgences as he sees fit. This power can be exercised directly by the Pope or through his priests who in turn have power to alleviate, shorten or terminate the sufferings. It is, of course, impossible but that power of this kind should be abused even in the hands of the best men. Vested in the hands of ordinary men, as generally must be the case, or in the hands of mercenary and wicked men as has too often happened, the abuses were bound to be appalling. The evils that have flowed from this doctrine, and which are its inevitable consequences, make it abundantly clear that it cannot be of divine origin.

The more satisfaction one makes while living, the less remains to be atoned for in purgatory. One of the most convenient and acceptable forms of service that can be rendered, of course, is the gift of money or property. The priest is authorized to accept the gift and to offer the prayer for the alleviation of suffering or the deliverance of the soul. The result, particularly among ignorant and uneducated people, has been that the Church sells salvation for money, not outwardly and directly but in the practical working out of the system.

It is safe to say that no other doctrine of the Church of Rome, unless it be that of auricular confession, has done so much to pervert the gospel or to enslave the people to the priesthood. Every year millions of dollars are paid to obtain relief from this imagined suffering. No exact figures are available, but it clearly constitutes a primary source of income. In contrast with the custom in Protestant churches, in which itemized financial statements of income and expenses are usually issued yearly, Roman Catholic church finances are kept secret, no kind of a balance sheet or budget ever being published which would show where their money comes from, how much it amounts to, or how it is used.

The doctrine of purgatory has sometimes been referred to as "the gold mine of the priesthood," since it is the source of such lucrative income. The Roman Church might well say, "By this craft we have our wealth."

A low mass for the benefit of a soul in purgatory costs a minimum of one dollar; a high mass costs from five to ten dollars; a solemn high mass (three priests, sung) costs twenty-five to thirty-five dollars. Prices vary somewhat in the different dioceses and according to the ability of the parishioners to pay. The more masses said the better for an agonizing soul. People with property are sometimes urged to leave thousands of dollars to provide for prayers and masses to be said perpetually for them after they die. It is due in no small measure to this doctrine that the Roman Catholic Church is able to build costly cathedrals, monasteries and convents even in regions where the people are comparatively poor. The practical working out of the system has been seen when in several countries, e. g., France, Italy, England, and Mexico, a disproportionately large part of the property fell into the hands of the Roman Catholic Church and had to be confiscated by the government to redress the economic situation.

The doctrine of purgatory represents God as a respecter of persons, which the Bible says He is not. Because of money a rich man can leave more for prayers and masses and so pass through purgatory and into heaven more speedily than many a poor man who may have more to commend him in God's sight. The Bible teaches that God's judgment is based on character alone, not on outward circumstances of wealth, position or social standing. This doctrine turns to commercial gain the remorse of immortal souls and the dearest affections of the bereaved for their departed relatives and friends, and prolongs indefinitely the hold of the priest over the guilty fears and hopes of people which

otherwise would end at death. People who sincerely believe
that they are to suffer or that their loved ones are suffering such pains will do almost anything to provide relief.

But just at this point a serious question arises: If the
Pope, or the priests acting for him, really has the power to
shorten or modify or terminate the sufferings of a soul in
purgatory, why does he not, if he is a good man, render
that service willingly and without pay? Why should he be
so insistent on the receipt of money before he renders that
service? If any one of us had that power and refused to
exercise it except after the payment of money he would be
considered cruel and unChristian, — which indeed he
would be. By all Christian standards that should be a service rendered freely and willingly by the Church to its
people. The insistence on a money transaction shows
clearly the purpose for which the doctrine was invented.
Practical experience has shown that few doctrines bring
forth worse fruit than this in the life of the church. A
mere reference to the days of Tetzel, Luther, and the great
Protestant Reformation, not to mention present day conditions in the Roman Catholic countries in southern Europe
and Latin America where that church has had undisputed
control for centuries, is sufficient to illustrate this point.

Since none but actual saints escape the pains of purgatory, this doctrine gives to the death and funeral of the
Roman Catholic a dreadful and repellent aspect. Under the
shadow of such a doctrine death is not, as in evangelical
Protestantism, the coming of Christ to take His loved one
home, but the ushering of the shrinking soul into a place
of unspeakable torture.

In opposition to the doctrine of purgatory we assert that
the whole idea that any person can make satisfaction to
divine justice for the sins of the dead is unscriptural and
of pagan origin. Belief that one could maintain contact
with the dead, and that he could influence them for good
or bad, has been an element in several of the pagan religions. When the Israelites came into the land of Canaan

Moses strictly charged them that they were not to follow the customs of the land in making gifts to or sacrificing for the dead, nor were they to allow any marks to be made in their flesh to appease or facilitate contact with the spirits of the dead. In Deut. 26:13,14 we read: "And thou shalt say before Jehovah thy God, I have put away the hallowed things [objects of heathen veneration and worship] out of my house . . . . I have not eaten thereof in my mourning, neither have I put away thereof, being unclean, nor given thereof for the dead." And further: "Ye shall not make cuttings in your flesh for the dead, nor print any marks upon you: I am Jehovah," Lev. 19:28. The Roman Catholic practice of gifts for the dead and prayers to the dead — to Mary and certain of the saints — is not far removed, if indeed it is removed at all, from such customs.

That the doctrine is unscriptural can be easily shown. The Bible says nothing about any such place as purgatory. The redeemed soul goes not to any midway station between earth and heaven, but directly to heaven. It needs no purgatorial process of cleansing for it is cleansed not with human merit but with the perfect righteousness of Christ, — in Paul's words, "not having a righteousness of mine own, even that which is of the law, but that which is through faith in Christ, the righteousness which is from God by faith," Phil. 3:9. Christ has done all that is necessary for our salvation. Faith in His finished work is the only thing that ever can or ever will save a sinner from hell. His death on the cross was sufficient to "purge" all our sins without the need of "purg"-atory. "It is appointed unto men once to die, and after this" — not a long purifying process, not an arduous education toward better things, but — the "judgment," Heb. 9:27. When Jesus said to the thief on the cross, "Today shalt thou be with me in Paradise," Luke 23:43, the clear inference was that at his death he would go immediately to heaven. Paul anticipated no purgatory, but said that to depart was to be with Christ and that it was far better. Nor is there any transfer from one realm to another after death. Those who go to the place of outer darkness cannot cross from that sphere to the other, — "between us and you there is a great gulf fixed, that they that would cross from hence to you may not be able, and that none may cross over from thence to us," Luke 16:26.

Furthermore, as Dr. Augustus H. Strong has said:

"Suffering has in itself no reforming power. Unless accompanied by special renewing influences of the Holy Spirit, it only hardens and embitters the soul. We have no Scriptural evidence that such influences of the Spirit are exerted, after death, upon the still impenitent; but abundant evidence, on the contrary, that the moral condition in which death finds men is their condition forever . . . . To the impenitent and rebellious sinner the motive must come, not from within, but from without. Such motives God presents by His Spirit in this life; but when this life ends and God's Spirit is withdrawn, no motives to repentance will be presented. The soul's dislike for God [we may even say, the sinner's hatred for God] will issue only in complaint and resistance."[22]

Roman Catholicism is to be thought of not as a pure type, but as a badly deformed type, of Christianity. It has become a religious totalitarianism, claiming authority over its subject not only as to what they may read or hear or do in this life, but also claiming authority to admit souls to or exclude them from heaven as they meet or fail to meet the demands of the Church for confession and penance. Professing to believe in the authority of the Bible, it has placed along side of the Bible as of equal authority a group of spurious writings known as the Apocrypha, and also a large collection of Church council decrees and papal proclamations, and it is almost exclusively from these latter sources that it derives its doctrine of purgatory. Three Scripture references are cited, but no one of them has any real bearing on the doctrine. They are: (the words of John

22. *Op. cit.*, p. 1041.

the Baptist concerning Christ) "He shall baptize you in the Holy Spirit and in fire," Matt. 3:11; "If any man's work shall be burned, he shall suffer loss; but he himself shall be saved; yet so as through fire," I Cor. 3:15; and, "And on some have mercy, who are in doubt; and some save, snatching them out of the fire," Jude 22,23. Surely this is indeed a very light cord on which to hang so heavy a weight.

The primary support for the doctrine of purgatory is found in II Maccabees 12:39-45, a Jewish book written after the close of the Old Testament canon and before the birth of Christ. That, of course, is an apocryphal book, and therefore is not acknowledged by Protestants as having any authority. In order to show how flimsy the evidence is for this important Roman Catholic doctrine we quote those verses in full:

"And the day following Judas came with his company, to take away the bodies of them that were slain, and to bury them with their kinsmen, in the sepulchres of their fathers. And they found under the coats of the slain some of the donaries of the idols of Jamnia, which the law forbiddeth to the Jews: so that all plainly saw, that for this cause they were slain. Then they all blessed the just judgment of the Lord, who had discovered the things that were hidden. And so betaking themselves to prayers, they besought him, that the sin which had been committed might be forgotten. But the most valiant Judas exhorted the people to keep themselves from sin, forasmuch as they saw before their eyes what had happened, because of the sins of those that were slain. And making a great gathering, he sent twelve thousand drachms of silver to Jerusalem for a sacrifice to be offered for the sins of the dead, thinking well and religiously concerning the resurrection. For if he had not hoped that they that were slain should rise again, it would have seemed superfluous and vain to pray for the dead. And because he considered that they who had fallen asleep with godliness, had great grace laid up for them. It is therefore a holy and wholesome thought to

pray for the dead that they may be loosed from sins."
(Douay Version.)

But those verses really do not teach the doctrine at all.
Furthermore, from the Roman Catholic viewpoint they
prove too much, for they teach the possible salvation of
soldiers who had died in the mortal sin of idolatry, and
that contradicts other Roman Catholic doctrine. Commenting on those verses Dr. R. Laird Harris, in a very helpful
little booklet, "Fundamental Protestant Doctrines," says:

"As one reads this statement one wonders whether one
who never heard of purgatory would learn about it from
this passage. The word purgatory does not occur in the
passage. It is merely stated that Judas Maccabeaus 'sent
into Jerusalem to offer a sacrifice for sin.' It is then said
that in this he 'took thought for a resurrection.' This says
nothing about helping poor souls to go from purgatory to
heaven, but simply looks forward to the resurrection of the
dead. How is it possible to build an argument for purgatory on such a passage as this!"

As indicated earlier, there is surprisingly little revealed
in Scripture concerning the intermediate state. This has
led some to resort to conjecture and imagination to fill out
the picture that revelation has given only in the barest out-
line. Hence we get, on the one hand, the Seventh-day Ad-
ventist doctrine of soul sleep between death and the resurrection, and on the other and at the opposite extreme the
Roman Catholic doctrine of purgatory, — for neither of
which is there any real Scriptural proof.

The Roman Catholic theologian Newman cites this doctrine as one of the clearest instances of "development"
from a slight Scriptural germ. But in reality it is an instance of the development from a germ of that which was
never in it to begin with, — as if from a mustard seed
one could develop an oak tree.

In defense of this doctrine Roman Catholics lay considerable stress upon the fact that the custom of praying for
the dead prevailed early and long in the church. Such

prayers, it is said, take for granted that the dead need our prayers, that they are not immediately in heaven. But, as we have pointed out in an earlier section, praying for the dead is a superstitious practice entirely without Scripture support. That was one of the early corruptions introduced into the Church from heathenism. It will not do to argue from one corruption to support another.

This much can be said for the doctrine: The term "purge," from which the word "purgatory" is derived, comes from Scripture, — that is, from the King James Version. But the following verses make it clear that the *true* purg(e)atory is not after death but in this present life: "Lo, this hath touched thy lips; and thine iniquity is taken away, and thy sin purged," Is. 6:7; "Purge me with hyssop, and I shall be clean: Wash me, and I shall be whiter than snow," Ps. 51:7; "And he shall sit as a refiner and purifier of silver: and he shall purify the sons of Levi, and purge them as gold and silver, that they may offer unto the Lord an offering in righteousness," Mal. 3:3; "Every branch in me that beareth not fruit he taketh away; and every branch that beareth fruit, he purgeth it, that it may bring forth more fruit," John 15:2. In each of these verses, however, the American Standard Version uses another word instead of "purge": i.e., forgive, purify, refine, and cleanse.

One thing that has given the doctrine of purgatory a certain amount of plausibility is the fact that we all are sinners and none attain perfect holiness in this life, while heaven is a place of perfect holiness where nothing evil can enter. The question naturally arises, How is the soul cleansed of the last remnants of sin before it enters heaven? Since this deals with something that is outside the realm of our experience it might seem reasonable to believe that there would be a place of further purification. In this case the Bible is our only trustworthy source of information. But a careful examination of all the passages relating to this subject shows that there are only two

abodes for the dead: a heaven for the saved, and a hell for
the lost. And in response to the question as to how the
Christian is made ready for heaven, the Bible teaches that
perfect righteousness is not to be had by any process at
all, but only through faith in Christ. We are "not justified
by the works of the law but through faith in Jesus Christ,"
Gal. 2:16. As expressed in the Westminster Confession:
"The souls of believers are at their death made perfect in
holiness." And if it be doubted that holiness can be attained in a single moment, let it be remembered that re-
covery from disease is ordinarily a process, but that when
Christ said, "I will; be thou made clean," even the leper
was cleansed in an instant (Matt. 8:3).

History of the doctrine. The germ of what afterward
grew into the doctrine of purgatory is to be found in the
idea of a purification by fire after death among the ancients
long before the time of Christ, particularly among the
people of India and Persia. It was a familiar idea to the
Egyptian and later to the Greek and Roman mind. It was
taken up by Plato and found expression in his philosophy.
He taught that perfect happiness after death was not possible until one had made satisfaction for his sins, and that
if his sins were too great his suffering would have no end.
Following the conquests of Alexander the Great, Greek influence spread through all the countries of western Asia,
including Palestine. We have seen that it found expression
in II Maccabees. The Rabbis came to teach that by means
of sin offerings children could alleviate the sufferings of
deceased parents. Later Jewish speculation divided the under-world into two abodes, — Paradise, a place of happiness, and Gehenna, a place of torment.

We need only to read church history to discover how
this doctrine developed by slow processes into its present
form. In the early Christian era, following the Apostolic
age, the writings of Marcion and the Shepherd of Hermas
(second century) set forth the first statement of a doctrine of purgatory, alleging that Christ after His death on

the cross went to the under-world and preached to the spirits in prison (I Peter 3:19) and led them in triumph to heaven. Prayers for the dead appear in the early Christian liturgies and imply the doctrine since they suggest that the state of the dead is not yet fixed. Origen, the most learned of the early church fathers (died, 254 A. D.), taught, first, that a purification by fire was to take place after the resurrection, and second, a universal restoration, a purifying fire at the end of the world through which all men and angels were to be restored to favor with God. The priestly conception of the Christian ministry was introduced probably as early as 200 A. D., and with it came the idea that the sacrament of the mass availed for the dead.

In the writings of Augustine (died, 430 A. D.) the doctrine was first given definite form, although he himself expressed doubt about some phases of it. It was, however, not until the sixth century that it received formal shape at the hands of Gregory the Great, who held the papal office 590-604 A. D. Thereafter eschatology entered on what we may call its mythological phase, during the period of history known as the Dark Ages. The invisible world was divided into heaven, hell and purgatory, with the imagination attempting to portray as vividly as possible the topography and experiences of each region. The Protestant Reformation swept away those creations of terror and fancy, and reverted to the Scriptural antithesis of heaven and hell.

The following paragraph by Dr. Charles Hodge shows the influence that this doctrine had in the lives and thinking of all classes of people during that period:

"It was Gregory the Great who consolidated the vague and conflicting views circulating through the Church, and brought the doctrine into such shape and into such connection with the discipline of the Church, as to render it the effective engine of government and income, which it has ever since remained. From this time onward through all the Middle Ages, purgatory became one of the promi-

inent and consistently reiterated topics of public discussion. It took firm hold of the popular mind. The clergy
from the highest to the lowest, and the different orders
of monks vied with each other in their zeal in its inculca-
tion, and in the marvels which they related of spiritual
apparitions, in support of the doctrine. They contended
fiercely for the honor of superior power of redeeming souls
from purgatorial pains. The Franciscans claimed that the
head of their order descended annually into purgatory, and
delivered all the brotherhood who were there detained.
The Carmelites asserted that the Virgin Mary had promised that no one who died with the Carmelite scapulary upon their shoulders, should ever be lost. The chisel and pen-
cil of the artist were employed in depicting the horrors of
purgatory, as means of impressing the public mind. No
class escaped the contagious belief; the learned as well as
the ignorant; the high and the low; the soldier and the re-
cluse; the skeptic and the believer were alike enslaved.
From this slavery the Bible, not the progress of science,
has delivered all Protestants . . . . All experience proves
that infidelity is no protection against superstition. If men
will not believe the rational and true, they will believe the
absurd and false."[23]

Our conclusion after a rather extensive survey of the
whole doctrine of purgatory is that it is not in the Bible,
that it is rather an invention of men and contrary to what
the Bible teaches. Our sins are cleansed, not by any fires
in purgatory, but by the blood of Christ our Saviour. "The
blood of Jesus his Son cleanses us from all sin," I John 1:7,
— thereby eliminating once and for all any need for such a
horrible place as purgatory. We do not say that no person
who believes in purgatory can be a Christian. Experience
shows that Christians as well as unbelievers sometimes can
be very inconsistent, that they may accept without thinking it through a doctrine or theory that is contrary to what

23. Op. cit., III, p. 770.

the Bible teaches and to what their hearts know to be true. But how thankful we should be that we are not under the false teaching of a misguided church or priesthood that threatens us with torments of purgatory, that instead we have the assurance that at death we go directly to heaven and enter immediately into its joys!

7. Spiritualism

Another subject that has a direct bearing on the nature and activity of the spirits of the dead in the intermediate state is Spiritualism. Spiritualism is the belief that the spirits of the dead can and do communicate with the living, usually through a "medium" who is susceptible to their influences.

The more accurate term for this belief is "Spiritism." But the term "Spiritualism" has long been in common use and has come to a definite and well understood meaning. Consequently in this discussion we shall follow the generally accepted practice and refer to it as "Spiritualism."

The thing that gives Spiritualism its strongest appeal is its professed ability to secure messages from departed loved ones and, to a lesser extent, its professed ability to foretell future events. It is rather closely related to fortune telling, palmistry, astrology, etc. Its chief patrons are grief stricken relatives and those who are in distress of one kind or another, often those who are worried about what the future may bring. Broken-hearted mothers, desolate widows and fatherless children in their grief have sought some direct message, some ray of hope from the other world, and in that moment of grief or despair Spiritualism seems to offer an easy solution. Usually those who patronize the mediums are people whose Christian faith is weak, or who are not Christians at all. Instead of trustingly accepting and acting upon the information given in the Bible, which information is amply sufficient and clear for those who put their trust in God, they have undertaken to secure direct answers through the spiritualistic mediums.

It seems that a considerable majority of those who function as mediums are women. Usually a medium claims to
have a particular "control" spirit who answers questions
or secures information from the deceased. Sometimes the
medium professes to bring back the spirits for personal appearances and direct questioning. Deluded thousands, particularly in the larger cities, are asking the mediums for
bread, but instead are receiving stones. We have no hesitation in declaring, primarily on the basis of Scripture
teaching, that Spiritualism is a snare and a delusion. A
Christian cannot do other than reject unconditionally the
claims of Spiritualism to open up the unseen world and
bring back the spirits of the deceased.

There is no satisfactory proof that the mediums actually
do contact those spirits. The contact, if it is real, presumably is with evil spirits who impersonate the departed or
who profess to give information from them. There is good
reason to believe that all of the spiritualistic phenomena is
produced by the mediums themselves or by their helpers.
Even the most famous mediums have been detected in
fraud, and some of them have been exposed time and again
as morally bad characters. And if they cheat sometimes,
how do we know that they do not cheat all the time?

THE SPIRITS OF THE DEAD CANNOT RETURN

The Bible teaches that death causes a complete break
with all that belongs to this world. This is set forth in both
the Old Testament and the New. Job said, "I go whence
I shall not return, Even to the land of darkness and of the
shadow of death," 10:21; and again, "He that goeth down
to Sheol shall come up no more. He shall return no more
to his house, Neither shall his place know him any more,"
7:9,10. David said concerning his son who had died, "I
shall go to him, but he will not return to me," II Sam.
12:23. A great truth of the New Testament is that the
souls of believers are at their death made perfect in holi-

ness and that they go immediately to be with the Lord. Paul describes this as, "Absent from the body . . . at home with the Lord," II Cor. 5:8. In the parable of the rich man and Lazarus the rich man in Hades was by his own admission unable to communicate with his brothers, nor was such communication permissible or even possible under any circumstances. The saved go to heaven; the lost go to hell. Neither can have any further communications with this world. The dead are said to be "asleep," — a figure which implies that they have no further contact with this earthly life, and that it is therefore impossible for us to communicate with them.

Nowhere in the Bible is there anything to indicate that the dead do return to this earth, either in spirit or in physical bodies except by a miracle when God Himself sends them back on a special mission. Such special cases we find in the appearance of Samuel when Saul sought information from the witch at Endor, in the instances in which people were raised from the dead (resuscitations, we may call them, not resurrections), performed by Elijah and Elisha, by the Lord and by the Apostles in His name, and in the appearance of some of the saints immediately after the resurrection of Christ (Matt. 27:52,53). But the Bible teaches that apart from such divine interference death brings about a permanent separation between the living and the dead.

THE ATTEMPT TO COMMUNICATE WITH THE DEAD IS FORBIDDEN

Not only does the Bible teach that it is impossible for the living to communicate with the dead, but the attempt to effect such communication is strictly forbidden. God's command through Moses to the Children of Israel as they were about to enter the land of Palestine was: "When thou art come into the land which Jehovah thy God giveth thee, thou shalt not learn to do after the abomination of the nations. There shall not be found with thee any one that maketh his son or his daughter to pass through the fire, one that useth divination, one that practiceth augury, or an enchanter, or a sorcerer, or a charmer, or a consulter with a familiar spirit, or a wizard, or a necromancer [literally, one who inquires of the dead]. For whosoever doeth these things is an abomination unto Jehovah," Deut. 18:9-12. "Thou shalt not suffer a sorceress to live," Ex. 22:18. "And the soul that turneth unto them that have familiar spirits, and unto the wizards, to play the harlot after them, I will even set my face against that soul, and will cut him off from among his people," Lev. 20:6. Isaiah repeated the same warning: "And when they shall say unto you, Seek unto them that have familiar spirits and unto the wizards, that chirp and that mutter: should not a people seek unto their God? on behalf of the living should they seek unto the dead? To the law and to the testimony! if they speak not according to this word, surely there is no morning for them," Is. 8:19,20. The sure test for any professed teacher or prophet, says Isaiah, is: Does he speak according to the Word of God, according to "the law and the testimony?" What the Bible calls a "familiar spirit" is what spiritualists today call a "control," — a spirit that supposedly gives information to or controls a medium.

These Scriptural representations should be enough to deter any Christian from ever attempting to communicate with the dead. The Bible is sufficiently plain. The sins here named are those that go with heathen idolatry. Those who consult fortune tellers, and those who go to spiritualistic seances and try to speak with the spirits of the dead, are guilty of this sin.

Listen to the stern rebuke that God delivered through the prophet Elijah to the apostate Ahaziah, king of Israel: "Is it because there is no God in Israel, that ye go to inquire of Baalzebub, the God of Ekron?" II Kings 1:3. How shameful that those whose faith should be in the true God should in their ignorance and impatience turn to such practices!

God in His word has seen fit to give us an abundance of reliable information about Himself, the way of salvation, and life beyond the grave. The resurrection of Christ is designed expressly to give the Christian the answer to the question concerning the reality of the future life. Some one has wisely said, "I do not know what the future holds, but I know the One who holds the future." Why should a Christian go to the false cults and to such shady characters as the fortune tellers to learn of the future? Or why should any one go to those sources for any kind of information or help? The only reason that spiritualistic mediums and fortune tellers continue to flourish and that people continue to pay out considerable sums of money for their "services" is, first of all, a tragic lack of spiritual understanding; secondly, the sheer gullibility of those who patronize them; and, thirdly, a certain amount of superstition in the make-up of a large number of people (even in many who refuse to acknowledge it openly), which causes all alleged supernatural phenomena to appear mysterious and which in turn makes it easy for them to believe there may be something to the claims of the spiritualists.

Dr. John R. Rice has recently said (and in this we agree with him fully): "It ought to be apparent to anyone who gives it a second thought that anyone who pretends to be able to foretell the future is a wicked fraud. Consider for a moment. If any foretuneteller could genuinely foretell the future, why should he or she need to open a dingy little office and collect money from the gullible poor to make a living? If a fortuneteller could foretell the price of any trading stock on the stock market next week, he could be rich over night. There are plenty of bankers, investors, industrial leaders, who would pay enormous sums for sure knowledge on such matters. If any fortuneteller could tell for certain how any big league baseball game would turn out, he could cash in. If he could tell which horse will win on any famous race course, he could make thousands. If he could tell what man would be elected to the presidency, or to a governorship, or any senate race, he could make unlimited money from that knowledge. If any fortune-teller could tell when war would come, when prices would go up or down, whether it will rain in a certain area at a needed time, that one could make plenty of money. The simple fact is that anybody who claims to be able to tell what will happen in the future, if he could prove the matter beyond doubt, could make millions of dollars out of the knowledge, and would not be in the poor, shabby business that he is in. Fortunetelling is a fraud, a deliberate, wicked, criminal fraud. And people who patronize fortunetellers are guilty of folly and of encouraging wickedness."[24]

TENETS OF SPIRITUALISM

Spiritualistic meetings are often given a religious setting. In some places they have their "churches," and make use of Scripture readings, appropriate hymns and music, and even prayer. This tends to provide a congenial atmosphere and to break down any reserve or prejudice on the part of those who are members of established churches. But the whole movement is un-Christian and anti-Christian, utterly subversive of the entire Christian system. First of all, it denies the inspiration of the Scriptures and seeks to lower the Bible to the level of other books. It denies the Deity of Christ and presents him as, of all things, a *medium!* and intimates that His supernatural powers were the same in kind as those exercised by present day mediums. It indignantly rejects the idea of His atonement as a satisfaction to divine justice for sin, and asserts that salvation is a matter of personal merit. Through it there runs a tendency toward universalism. It denies the doctrines of the Trinity and the Holy Spirit, the existence of hell and the personality of the Devil, making the Devil an abstract

24. *The Sword of the Lord*, Sept. 24, 1954.

principle of evil. One writer says, "There is no Devil and there are no evil spirits." It treats lightly the doctrine of sin and the need for forgiveness.

Perhaps the most wide-spread and popular form of occultism in our country today is astrology. Astrology is a pseudo-science which professes to interpret the influence of the stars on human affairs and so to foretell the future. It is pure fiction and untruth.

There are, of course, many things about the future that we do not know, for it has pleased God not to reveal them to us, and it is not our place to pry into knowledge that He has forbidden. In regard to forbidden knowledge it is well to remember that when our first parents were in their unfallen state there was a tree in the garden that held a secret, a secret of the knowledge of good and evil, and they were warned that the knowledge it contained was not for them. In prying into the knowledge of good and evil they would become the victims of evil. But, heedless of the warning, they determined to investigate. The result proved fatal to the human race. They unfolded a mystery that condemned them body and soul. Their inquisitive disobedience gained for them nothing, but destroyed everything that they held dear. In our day those who hanker after forbidden knowledge, knowledge which they imagine can be gained through the services of a spiritualistic medium, show what a complete lack of appreciation they have for Christian truth.

In the parable of the rich man and Lazarus the rich man is reminded that his brothers had the writings of Moses and the prophets, and that they therefore had all the information they needed. We who live in the light of the completed New Testament have a much fuller revelation, and we have the promise that the Holy Spirit will guide us into the truth if we diligently seek it. Surely we have much less need for the spirits of the dead to come back and inform us regarding conditions in the next world. Any movement that claims that departed spirits are free to do what the

Bible says they cannot do thereby labels itself as anti-Christian through and through.

RESULTS OBTAINED BY THE USE OF MAGIC

We do not pretend to know the answer to all of the Spiritualistic phenomena. Some of it seems quite weird and even supernatural to the average layman. We believe, however, that in the main the results are obtained through the use of magic, — that is, slight of hand, technical manipulations that are so rapid or so concealed that they escape the eye of the observer, — and that however mysterious the results may appear to the uninitiated they are obtained through purely natural means. On different occasions we have seen skilled magicians mystify an audience with one trick after another; yet we do not believe there was anything supernatural about their accomplishments, and most of them are frank enough to admit as much.

So much trickery and fraud on the part of the mediums has been exposed that entirely apart from the condemnations in Scripture the whole movement has been brought under deep suspicion. Dr. William E. Biederwolf made a considerable study of Spiritualism and its methods, and his conclusion was that "A bigger set of liars and fakers never lived than the majority of these mediums and clairvoyants and clairaudients and slate-writers and table-tippers and other ghostly manipulators." — *Spiritualism*, p. 5. The conditions on which mediums usually insist, such as a darkened room, a select group of people, obedience to particular instructions, etc., make it extremely difficult for those who are not familiar with magic phenomena to detect the trickery.

COLLUSION WITH EVIL SPIRITS?

Another explanation given by some who have studied the spiritualistic phenomena is that the alleged supernaturalistic events are caused by evil spirits. Quite clearly it cannot be of divine origin, nor produced by the holy angels, for it is condemned in Scripture. We know that evil spirits do exist, and that they have access to this world. Both the Old Testament and the New make that abundantly clear. An evil spirit came upon king Saul, I Sam. 16:14; 18:10; also upon the prophets who prophesied before king Ahab, I Kings 22:21-23. Demon possession was a well known phenomenon in New Testament times. On numerous occasions Jesus cast out evil spirits from those who were possessed. Various physical afflictions were attributed to demon possession. We are told, for instance, "Then was brought unto him one possessed with a demon, blind and dumb: and he healed him, insomuch that the dumb man spake and saw," Matt. 12:22. An epileptic boy was cured when the demon was cast out, Matt. 17:14-18. A woman who for eighteen years had been bowed so that she could not lift herself up, was healed, concerning whom Jesus said, "Ought not this woman, being a daughter of Abraham, whom Satan had bound, lo, these eighteen years, to have been loosed from this bond," Luke 13:10-17. The Apostle Paul, writing to the church in Thessalonica, expressed his desire to visit them and said that he and Timothy would have come to them once and again, but, he adds, "Satan hindered us," I Thess. 2:18.

It may be that many of the temptations and misfortunes that befall us — diseases, accidents, broken bones, property losses, even death — are caused by evil spirits or by the Devil himself. Our eyes cannot see them because they are spirits entirely apart from any material body. But their influence in the spiritual realm may be as real as certain other forces in the material world which also are unseen, such as gravity, magnetism, radio or television waves. In Job's case the Devil did not show himself directly, but worked through the forces of nature, that is, through second causes. The Sabeans (bandits) stole Job's oxen and killed his servants; the lightning killed his sheep; the Chaldeans stole his camels; a great wind from the desert blew down the house where his sons and daughters were feast-

ing and killed them; and Job himself fell a victim of painful boils.   From the human viewpoint all of these things
seemed to happen in the regular course of nature. Job apparently had no other idea than that they were natural hap-
penings.   But the account tells us that the Devil had been
given permission to tempt Job through these trials, that for
Job the trials were disciplinary in character, and that the
Devil could not touch Job until he was given permission
and then could cause affliction only within prescribed limits. If such likewise is the case with many of our seeming
misfortunes, we may be sure that they occur only with
God's permission, and that as in Job's case they eventually
are to be overruled for good.

This does not substantiate Spiritualism, for there is no
proof that the mediums or any one else actually has power
to contact the spirits or to influence them in any way. If
the possibility is granted that the phenomena are caused
in part at least by spirits, it means that the spirits who
manifest themselves at the seances, or who give the mediums information which it seems would be impossible to
secure through ordinary human channels, are not the spirits
of loved ones at all, but spirits from the world of darkness,
perhaps in some instances the Devil himself. In any event
no one ever finds the secret of true happiness or the way to
permanent success and prosperity by patronizing the mediums or fortune tellers. The strong denunciations against
necromancy given in Scripture are intended to safeguard
humanity against those deceptions.

SAUL AND THE WITCH OF ENDOR

The one event in Scripture most often cited by Spiritualists as supporting their claims that departed spirits can
communicate with the living is Saul's visit to the witch of
Endor.   This is recorded in I Sam. 28:3-25.   We believe,
however, that a careful examination of this passage will
show that instead of supporting the claim it really contains
a strong refutation of it.

Let us recall the story. The old prophet Samuel was dead. Saul, the king of Israel, had gone from bad to worse and was a God-forsaken man. The Philistines were marshalling their armies against him. The ordinary channels of revelation were closed to him because of his willful disobedience, — "Jehovah answered him not, neither by dreams, nor by Urim, nor by prophets." The impending battle with the Philistines filled him with fear, and he did not know where to turn. He thought of Samuel and longed for some word from him as of old. He knew that those who dealt with familiar spirits were reputed to be able to call up the dead. Though earlier in his reign Saul had abolished under penalty of death all who acted as mediums, wizards, necromancers, etc., now in his despair and superstition he seeks out one who was practicing illegally at the town of Endor, — much as a present day ruler who had outlawed liquor might go in search of a bootlegger.

Disguising himself, Saul went to this woman. She reminded him that Saul had forbidden such practice under penalty of death. But after receiving a solemn promise that no punishment would come to her she asked, "Whom shall I bring up unto thee?" Saul asked that Samuel might be brought up. The story continues:

"And when the woman saw Samuel, she cried with a loud voice; and the woman spake to Saul, saying, Why hast thou deceived me? for thou art Saul. And the king said unto her, Be not afraid: for what seest thou? And the woman said unto Saul, I see a god coming up out of the earth. And he said unto her, What form is he of? And she said, An old man cometh up; and he is covered with a robe. And Saul perceived that it was Samuel, and he bowed with his face to the ground, and did obeisance.

"And Samuel said to Saul, Why hast thou disquieted me, to bring me up? And Saul answered, I am sore distressed; for the Philistines make war against me, and God is departed from me, and answereth me no more, neither by prophets, nor by dreams: therefore I have called thee, that

thou mayest make known unto me what I shall do. And
Samuel said, Wherefore then dost thou ask of me, seeing
Jehovah is departed from thee, and is become thine adver-
sary? And Jehovah hath done unto thee as he spake by me:
and Jehovah hath rent the kingdom out of thy hand, and
given it to thy neighbor, even to David. Because thou obey-
est not the voice of Jehovah, and didst not execute his fierce
wrath upon Amalek, therefore hath Jehovah done this
thing unto thee this day. Moreover Jehovah will deliver
Israel also with thee into the hand of the Philistines; and
tomorrow shalt thou and thy sons be with me: Jehovah
will deliver the host of Israel also into the hand of the
Philistines. Then Saul fell straightway his full length upon the earth, and was sore afraid, because of the words of
Samuel."

That is the story. Saul resorted to what we call a spiritualistic medium, and God gave him a message of doom, —
defeat for the army, pillaging of the country, and death for
himself and his sons. As we read this story two questions
come to mind: (1) Was it really Samuel who appeared and
spoke to Saul? and (2) If it was Samuel, did the woman
really possess the power to call him up?

In regard to the first question, everything in the story
indicates that Samuel actually did appear and that he spoke
to Saul. We are told that the woman saw Samuel (vs. 12),
that Saul perceived that it was Samuel (vs. 14), that Samuel spoke to Saul (vs. 15), that Samuel sternly rebuked
Saul (vss. 16-19), and that Saul was afraid because of the
words of Samuel (vs. 20). It is definitely stated that Samuel spoke to Saul. All of this is given in a straight forward, historical narrative, and there is no hint anywhere
in the entire story that it was either the woman or an evil
spirit impersonating Samuel.

In regard to the second question, we cannot believe that
the woman actually had power over the spirit of Samuel
to cause him to appear at her beck and call. Such belief
would be contrary to the general teaching of Scripture on

this subject. It seems clear that something happened that the woman herself had not expected. She evidently had expected to do what she usually did, — go into a trance (real or pretended), impersonate Samuel, and so fool her visitors. But when a spirit actually did appear, rising as a wraith from the earth and terrible in its majesty, she was the most surprised person of all. She was, if we may use the expression, literally scared out of her wits, and screamed, — "cried with a loud voice." If she had been what she pretended to be, a medium able to call up such spirits from the grave, this appearance should have been only routine and she should in fact have expected it to happen. But here was something entirely different from the usual experience of a medium.

From the time that Samuel appeared, the woman had no further part in the affair except as a spectator. It seems clear that in this instance God actually sent back the prophet Samuel, that He *superseded the seance* and used this as an occasion to pronounce judgment upon the wilfully disobedient king Saul. In the parallel account in I Chronicles 10:13,14 the element of Saul's disobedience is particularly stressed: "So Saul died for his trespass which he committed against Jehovah, because of the word of Jehovah, which he kept not; and also for that he asked counsel of one that had a familiar spirit, to inquire thereby, and inquired not of Jehovah: therefore he slew him, and turned the kingdom to David the Son of Jesse." Surely this cannot be taken as Scripture in support of Spiritualism.

> "Oh, the road to Endor is the oldest road,
>   And the craziest road of all.
> Straight it runs to the witch's abode
>   As it did in the days of Saul,
> And nothing has changed of the sorrow in store
>   For such as go down on the road to Endor."
>   —Rudyard Kipling

Origin Of The Spiritualistic Movement

Spiritualistic phenomena in one form or another go back very far in history. But modern Spiritualism as we know it really began with the Fox family, in a humble farm home, in Hydesville, New York, in 1848. The house occupied by the Fox family was regarded by the community as a haunted house. Over a period of months the family had been annoyed with mysterious rappings. M'Clintock and Strong's *Encyclopedia of Biblical, Theological and Ecclesiastical Literature* gives the following account:

"In the month of January, 1848, the noises assumed the character of distinct knockings at night in the bedrooms, sounding sometimes as from the cellar below, and resembling the hammering of a shoemaker. These knocks produced a tremulous motion in the furniture and even in the floor. The children (Margaret, aged 12 years, and Kate, aged 9 years) felt something heavy, as of a dog, lie on their feet when in bed; and Kate felt, as it were, a cold hand pressed upon her face. Sometimes the bedclothes were pulled off. Chairs and the dining table were moved from their places. Raps were made on doors as they stood close to them, but on suddenly opening them no one was visible. On the night of March 31, 1848, the knockings were unusually loud, whereupon Mr. Fox tried the sashes, to see if they were shaken by the wind. Kate observed that the knockings in the room exactly answered the rattle made by her father with the sash. Thereupon she snapped her fingers and exclaimed, 'Here, old Splitfoot, do as I do.' The rap followed. This at once arrested the mother's attention. 'Count ten,' she said. Ten strokes were distinctly given. 'How old is my daughter Margaret?' Twelve strokes. 'And Kate?' 'Nine.' Other questions were answered. When she asked if it was a man, no answer. Was it a spirit? It rapped. A number of questions were put to the spirit, which replied by knocks that it was that of a traveling salesman, who had been murdered by the then tenant, John C. Bell, for his property. The peddler had never been seen afterward; and on the floor being dug up, the remains of a human body were found."

That, in brief, was the beginning of modern Spiritualism. Margaret and Kate Fox were taken in charge by an older sister, Leah, who sponsored and exhibited them on entertainment platforms. Both went on to become famous mediums. During the immediately following years the movement had an incredibly rapid growth. A corps of workers and lecturers took up the movement and popularized it, and it spread throughout New York and the New England states, as far west as St. Louis, into Canada, and even across the Atlantic to England.

Forty years later, after the movement had attained world wide attention, the Fox sisters explained the method by which they had produced the spirit phenomena. They acknowledged that their results were obtained by trickery and fraud. Each repudiated her connection with the whole movement. Margaret arranged for a public demonstration in New York and began her repudiation with these words:

"I am here tonight as one of the founders of Spiritualism to denounce it as an absolute falsehood from beginning to end, as the flimsiest of superstitions, the most wicked blasphemy known to the world." But that was as far as she got. Her enemies in the audience created such a disturbance that, due in part to the state of nervous exhaustion she was in, she could not go on. But a New York newspaper, the *World*, under date of October 22, 1888, carried this report:

"But if her tongue had lost its power her preternatural toe-joint had not. A plain wooden stool or table, resting on four short legs and having the properties of a sounding board, was placed in front of her. Removing her shoe, she placed her right foot on this table. The entire house became breathlessly still, and was rewarded by a number of short, sharp raps — those mysterious sounds which have for more than forty years frightened and bewildered hundreds of thousands of people in this country and Europe. A committee consisting of three physicians taken from the audience then ascended the stage, and having made an examination of her foot during the process of the 'rappings,' unhesitatingly agreed that the sounds were made by the action of the first joint of her large toe."[25]

Charles W. Ferguson, author of a book dealing with various present-day cults, gives the following information concerning the Fox sisters during the period previous to their repudiation of the movement:

"Kate married and later gave up the profession of Spiritualism — joining her sister in its denunciation in 1888. An explorer, Dr. Elisha Kent Kane, became interested in Margaret and sought to induce her to give up the humbuggery — the term was used freely in his letters to her — and become his wife. He was, unfortunately for the match, the son of a wealthy family who resented his passion for one of the Fox sisters, and after many fervent letters to and from the arctic, they were forced to be content with a common law marriage. Soon after this Kane sailed for England, promising soon to return and claim his bride. But he died before the two ever met again. A child was born to Margaret Fox Kane, and she found herself without means of support. She drifted back into spiritualism, later began to drink heavily, and at last broke with Leah and entered the Roman Catholic Church. It was upon her return to America from abroad in 1888 that she made her startling recantation of the Spiritualistic doctrine and gave such convincing proof of its fraudulence. For thirty years before her exposure, she lived in constant dread and fear of Leah."[26]

---

25. Quoted by Charles W. Ferguson, in *The Confusion of Tongues*, p. 26.
26. *The Confusion of Tongues*, p. 25.

HOUDINI'S ATTITUDE TOWARD SPIRITUALISM

Another phase of the Spiritualistic controversy that must not be overlooked and which in the opinion of the present writer probably is more important than any other except direct Scripture teaching, is the attitude taken toward it by the most famous magician that the world has yet produced, Mr. Harry Houdini.

A fact that gave special weight to Houdini's verdict was his unsurpassed knowledge of the whole field of magic and occultism and his ability to mystify a critical as well as a credulous audience.   Time and again he performed feats that the most meticulous observer considered impossible and which other magicians were not able to duplicate. Yet he made no claim to supernatural power. Rather he insisted that all of those feats were accomplished through purely natural means. He could do them because he knew magic. And that, declared Houdini, is precisely what the mediums do.

On repeated occasions Houdini exposed mediums who pretended to call forth the voices and spirits of the dead by other than purely physical means. He was on the committee set up by the *Scientific American magazine* to investigate spiritualistic phenomena, in connection with which an award of $2,500 was offered to any medium who could prove to the satisfaction of the committee that he — or she — actually could call forth the spirits of the dead. He repeatedly challenged mediums to meet him in debate before their own audiences, and his programs carried a "CHALLENGE TO ANY MEDIUM IN THE WORLD" to present "so-called psychical manifestations that I cannot reproduce or explain as being accomplished by natural means." He offered to donate as much as $10,000 to charity if his challenge were successfully met. But the award went unclaimed. After one of his programs the Providence *News* commented: "Houdini knows a few tricks himself and he knows them even better than the cleverest psychic frauds.

More power to Houdini to run the fakirs out of business."

For a short time in his early career Houdini had prac-
ticed as a medium and knew how most of their effects were
produced. He says later that he did not realize how wrong
it was to prey on the hopes and fears of the bereaved until
his own mother, whom he loved very dearly, died, and he
himself was grief-stricken. That experience caused him to
turn strongly against Spiritualism. In the opening paragraph of his book, *A Magician Among The Spirits*, published in 1924, he says:

"From my early career as a mystical entertainer I have
been interested in Spiritualism as belonging to the cat-
egory of mysticism, and as a side line to my own phase of
mystery shows. I have associated myself with mediums,
joining the rank and file and held seances as an independent
medium to fathom the truth of it all. At the time I appre-
ciated the fact that I surprised my clients, but while aware
of the fact that I was *deceiving* them I did not see or understand the seriousness of trifling with such sacred senti-
mentality and the baneful result which inevitably followed.
To me it was a lark. I was a mystifier and as such my am-
bition was being gratified and my love for a mild sensation
satisfied. After delving deep I realized the seriousness of
it all. As I advanced to riper years of experience I was
brought to a realization of the seriousness of trifling with
the hallowed reverences which the average human being
bestows on the departed, and when I personally became afflicted with similar grief I was chagrined that I should
ever have been guilty of such frivolity and for the first time
realized that it bordered on crime."

He continues: "It has been my life work to invent and
publicly present problems, the secrets of which not even
the members of the magical profession have been able to
discover, and the effects of which have proved as inexplicable to the scientists as any marvel of the mediums. My
record as a 'mystifier of mystifiers' qualifies me to look
below the surface of any mystery problem presented to me

and that with my eyes trained by thirty years of experience in the realm of occultism it is not strange that I view these so-called phenomena from a different angle than the ordinary layman or even the expert investigator. . . .

"I have accumulated one of the largest libraries in the world on mystic phenomena, Spiritualism, magic, witchcraft, demonology, evil spirits, etc., some of the material going back to 1489, and I doubt if anyone in the world has so complete a library on modern Spiritualism, but nothing I ever read concerning the so-called Spiritualistic phenomena has impressed me as genuine. . . . Mine has not been an investigation of a few days or weeks or months but one that has extended over thirty years and in that thirty years I have not found one incident that savored of the genuine. If there had been any real unalloyed demonstration to work on, one that did not reek of fraud, one that could not be reproduced by earthly powers, then there would be something for a foundation, but up to the present time everything that I have investigated has been the result of deluded brains or those which were actively and intimately willing to believe."

Houdini's contacts with Sir Conan Doyle, with whom he was on very friendly terms, were quite interesting. Doyle was a British author who, after the loss of a son in World War I, turned to Spiritualism and became one of its most enthusiastic advocates. Doyle became convinced that Houdini was himself a medium, capable of more-than-human actions. He declared that Houdini could perform some of his tricks only by "dematerializing" himself — that is, by dissolving his physical body — and "rematerializing" himself later. Houdini's reply to such statements was an unqualified declaration that he accomplished all of his escapes and other feats by purely physical means.

After a tour of England in which he gave many public performances, a British writer, J. Hewat McKenzie, President of the British College of Psychic Science, in a book entitled *Spirit Intercourse,* said:

"Houdini, called the 'Handcuff King,' who has so ably demonstrated his powers upon public-hall platforms is enabled by psychic power (though this he does not advertise), to open any lock, handcuff, or bolt that is submitted to him. He has been imprisoned within heavily barred cells, doubly and trebly locked, and from them all he escaped with ease. This ability to unbolt locked doors is undoubtedly due to his mediumistic powers, and not to any normal mechanical operation on the lock. The force necessary to shoot a bolt within a lock is drawn from Houdini the medium, but it must not be thought that this is the only means by which he can escape from his prison, for at times his body has been dematerialized and withdrawn" (p. 107).

In reply to this Houdini said: "As I am the one most deeply concerned in that charge I am also the best equipped to deny any such erroneous statements. I do claim to free myself from the restraint of fetters and confinement, but positively state that I accomplish my purpose purely by physical, not psychical means. The force necessary to 'shoot a bolt within a lock,' is drawn from Houdini the living human being and not a medium. My methods are perfectly natural, resting on natural laws of physics. I do not *dematerialize* or *materialize* anything; I simply control and manipulate natural things in a manner perfectly well known to myself, and thoroughly accountable for and adequately understandable (if not duplicable) by any person to whom I may elect to divulge my secrets. I hope to carry these secrets to the grave as they are of no material benefit to mankind, and if they should be used by dishonest persons they might become a serious detriment."[27]

Houdini pointed out that many of the marvels of scientific achievement, such as the radio, airplane, radium [and in our day we might add television, even in color and three dimensions, radar, and atomic energy], were at one time classed as impossible and would have been looked upon as

27. *A Magician Among the Spirits*, p. 211.

supernatural, if not as spiritual manifestations. Because a thing looks mysterious to one person does not necessarily mean that it would be considered supernatural or mystic if he had fuller information. Concerning one very baffling trick performed by a medium who supposedly was securely bound, Houdini said, "I have performed it regularly for thirty years without any supernatural power whatever."

The scheming of the mediums and fortune tellers to get bits of information, some of it relating to details of long past events that may have been forgotten by the client, and their skillful presentation of it in such a way as to give the impression that they have supernatural insight, is as devious as their tricks in the physical realm. They have sometimes worked for days or even weeks gathering detailed information from old letters, newspaper clippings, relatives, or former acquaintances. The success of the mediums and fortune tellers often times is aided by the uncritical attitude or even blind faith of those who go to them. "Distressed relatives," said Houdini, "catch at the least word which may remotely indicate that the spirit which they seek is in communication with them. One little sign even, which appeals to their waiting imagination, shatters all ordinary caution and they are convinced. Then they begin to accept all kinds of natural events as results of spirit intervention."

One of Houdini's most famous tricks was to have on the stage a large milk can filled with water, in which he would allow himself to be submerged, then the top would be put on and securely fastened with three locks and a chain. A curtain would then be drawn around the can, and within twenty seconds, while the people in the audience were still gasping with astonishment, he would appear from behind the curtain, his clothes dripping with water. This trick was accomplished by using a can from which the rivets that held the oval top part of the can to the sidewall had been removed and replaced with dummies, allowing the can to be manipulated from within so that the entire upper part came off as a unit, which of course left the locks and chain unmolested. The removed part could then be snapped back in place, and when the curtain was withdrawn the can appeared to the audience and to the men who had put the locks and chain on it never to have been opened. Another popular trick was that of escaping from a trunk that had been locked and tied with ropes, or from a wooden box that had been built on the platform by carpenters from the audience. The secret of the trunk escape was a sliding side panel that collapsed inward. When the box trick was performed the box would be built one night, with the escape to be made the second night. After the program he and his aids cleverly fixed a board so that it could be collapsed inward but with the alterations so concealed that they were not detected by the carpenters who the second night again would be invited to come on stage and verify that it was the same box they had built. During his career he invented dozens of tricks that had not been performed by other magicians. But through it all he insisted that his feats were accomplished through purely physical means.

Houdini's controversy with Spiritualism had to do primarily with its moral effects. "Spiritualism," he said, "touches every phase of human affairs and emotions, leaving in its wake a train of victims whose plight is frequently pathetic, sometimes ludicrous, often miserable and unfortunate, and who are always deluded. It is to these effects of Spiritualism which are so seldom considered that I wish to call the reader's attention" (p. 180). To any one who is interested in a thorough and well documented exposure of the mediums, Houdini's book, *A Magician Among The Spirits,* is especially recommended.

Our conclusions concerning the whole matter of Spiritualism are:

(1) It is impossible to communicate with the spirits of the dead.

(2) All spiritualistic practice is severely condemned in the Bible. It is therefore morally wrong for any one, and particularly for Christians, to have anything to do with it.

(3) The effect of Spiritualism is to lead people away from a right belief in God and in His Word.

(4) The spiritualistic phenomena in the seances is produced neither by departed human spirits, nor by evil spirits, but by deception and by the clever use of magic on the part of the mediums.

INDEX OF AUTHORS

INDEX OF SUBJECTS